Accelerating Business

How to Accelerate the Implementation and Adoption Rate of New Business Initiatives and Strategies

MICHAEL H. TAYLOR

iUniverse, Inc.
New York   Bloomington

iUniverse books may be ordered through booksellers or by contacting:

iUniverse
1663 Liberty Drive
Bloomington, IN 47403
www.iuniverse.com
1-800-Authors (1-800-288-4677)

Because of the dynamic nature of the Internet, any Web addresses or links contained in this book may have changed since publication and may no longer be valid. The views expressed in this work are solely those of the author and do not necessarily reflect the views of the publisher, and the publisher hereby disclaims any responsibility for them.

ISBN: 978-1-4401-7008-9 (sc)
ISBN: 978-1-4401-7009-6 (ebook)
ISBN: 978-1-4401-7010-2 (dj)

Printed in the United States of America

iUniverse rev. date: 8/6/2010

To Nancy, Graham, Clara, and Mathew

Accelerating Business

☑ A Systematic Approach to Elevate Change Management to Business Acceleration

☑ Not Only a Guiding Process, but Also a Handbook of Tips, from Experience, to Improve Acceptance and Adoption of New Ideas and Systems

☑ A Guide to Help Avoid Potential Pitfalls That Can Slow Down or Derail Success

☑ A Faster Road to Results without Speed-Associated Risk; Accelerated Implementation Does Not Have to Amplify Risk.

☑ Creating the Most Powerful and Sustainable Competitive Advantage—Agility

☑ Don't Simply Manage Strategy Implementation and Business Change ...

... Accelerate It!

... Successfully!

Accelerating Business

Accelerating Business is an essential book for any leader who is implementing a new business strategy or introducing a change to the organization or who needs business initiatives to be successful faster.

This book will introduce you to the AIM approach, which outlines a clear process that enables you to drive change with fewer problems along the way.

Clear practical advice and tips helps with the big stuff and the small stuff.

Contents

Introduction

Competition, technology, the economy, and the increasing pace of business are creating unprecedented pressure on business leaders to implement new business plans faster, with little room for contingencies or risk of failure. After two decades of management, I have seen, and sometimes been part of, both implementation successes and implementation messes. This book is written from experience to provide tips and recommendations, as well as provide a structured approach to avoid common pitfalls during the implementation of new business initiatives. This book details the ingredients to help successfully accelerate business plan implementation and business change.

The Most Common Missing Link

It has been said that good news does not sell newspapers—bad news, or even better, a disaster, sells newspapers. So maybe we are accustomed to hearing bad news in the media. But if we look beyond the bias toward bad news, the headlines of failure in the business section are too frequent. There are some memorable topics that have failed to generate their expected results: new product introductions (the New Coke), outsourcing decisions (moving production to Asia), mergers and acquisitions (Daimler/Chrysler and AOL/Time-Warner), and technology initiatives (CRM), to name a few. Unfortunately, there are many less-publicized business-strategy flameouts that for one reason or another fail to generate the expected results. Is it because the strategy is wrong? Is it because we are overly optimistic when we make our projections? Is it because our analysis is weak? Often not. More often initiatives fail during implementation. The expected results are realistic, but somehow we can't attain them. If we could become better implementers, we would see more success. When do we want that success? Normally as quickly as possible. The desire for a fast finish frequently has the opposite effect. Fast-track implementation can create additional problems, promote just-make-do solutions, truncate the potential benefits with a less than adequate adoption, create confusion, generate cost overruns, and increase the risk of delays. We need to become better implementers to accelerate implementation with a higher degree of success and not let costs get out of control.

The implementation of a new business initiative, or for that matter, managing change in general, can be a complicated endeavor. The best business strategies and business plans can fizzle during implementation if not orchestrated and managed effectively. Managing the implementation of a new business approach is not a matter of giving orders and expecting "the troops" to follow commands. Rather, it is a complicated mixture of strategy, planning, management, motivation, and psychology. Now add the ever-present requirement—the need to implement it faster than ever before without sacrificing success.

Unfortunately, a lack of change-management expertise is all too common. To make matters worse, traditional change management is insufficient for the pace for today's business requirements. This is precisely the reason for the failure of many credible business plans.

There are a few key purposes for this book:

- to describe a structured approach, the AIM approach, that will help make business plan implementation smoother and faster without sacrificing success

- to share some common pitfalls and tips from experience that will elevate traditional change-management techniques to business acceleration

- to provide the foundation that can give your organization the competitive advantages of agility

Why Is This Important?

Agility is a competitive advantage. The only constant is change. Those who can make major changes quickly have agility. Agility is increasingly becoming the competitive advantage that propels firms to leadership positions in their industry. The accelerating pace of economic change in the world and the increased competitive intensity in many markets requires leading organizations to be agile so they can hang on to market share. The first to capitalize on a shift in the market or a new technology development has a distinct competitive advantage. Those same firms seem to also be able to capitalize on the next new development. What makes them so agile? It is more than having good "idea people." Those organizations are agile. They are accelerated implementers. They are proficient at managing change. They have a heightened readiness to adapt to changes that appear.

To remain ahead of competition, the pace of development is accelerating. It is frequently necessary to take bold strategic steps forward that invariably require major changes in your business model, organization, structure, go-to-market strategy, manufacturing or logistics philosophy, and more.

Now overlay on top of normal market dynamics the never-before-seen pace of technology advancements. Technology advancements are not necessarily complicated nuclear physics—they are often advancements at the shop-floor level or in the mainstream office environment. All these factors compound the need to become relatively proficient at thriving in an environment of change.

Agility and accelerated change management is an increasingly necessary core skill required by virtually every organization. This competitive advantage can be applied to simple improvements or situations of complex enterprise-wide restructuring.

The pace of increasing competitive pressure and technological advancements is driving more and larger-scale change than ever before. New systems or business structures that fundamentally change large portions of the business have the potential for large-scale disaster. The speed of implementation demanded is increasing the risk of failure. Change management is not the same as project management. Unlike project management, which has many decades of experience, installed discipline, professional experience, and best-practice sharing, change management is not as developed and as a result provides a platform for problems. Also, unlike project management, change management has not been a core skill developed by young managers as they matured into leadership positions.

In addition, the very pressures that are driving the increasing need to change quickly are also demanding improvements without interruptions in financial performance or disturbance to regular operations.

Why is this book important? This book is most likely categorized under the broad title of Change Management, and there are a number of good books on this broad topic on the bookshelves today. Most are from the strategic, leadership, or organizational-behavior perspective. Many of them are interesting, provide good insights, and have good anecdotal stories of one corporation or another, but few of them offer practical how-to advice or address the pressure for acceleration that is facing managers today. That is why I wrote this book. This is not a change-management textbook. This is a book written with the insights of experience, providing a structured approach focused on the ingredients necessary to successfully accelerate business plan implementation and business change.

Who Is This Book For?

If you are embarking on a new business plan or a new business strategy that requires people to do things differently …
OR
If you are making changes to a well-entrenched organization that you believe will find the changes difficult …
OR
If you are introducing ideas that will require some degree of culture change in your organization …
OR
If you are introducing changes that can possibly disrupt normal operations and you need to minimize the time of turmoil or the customer impact …
OR
If you are introducing a new system or new technology into your organization and you need a high degree of acceptance and adoption …
OR
If you are implementing new ideas in a complex organization—perhaps a large or widely decentralized organization …
OR
If you are introducing actions that must be completed quickly …
OR
If you need to have a fast switch-over …
OR
If the new ideas you are introducing have a high degree of risk and must be implemented with a high probability of success the first time …
OR
If you are in a fast-changing industry or facing a fast-changing market and you need to develop agility in your organization …

… then this book is for you.

If you recognize any of the factors mentioned above, then the systematic approach and the practical tips in this book will help.

The "lessons learned from experience" that are described throughout this book will also serve as a career-building skill set that we all should have.

An Introduction to *AIM*, the *Accelerated Implementation Model*

New business initiatives do not move forward on their own. Acceptance and adoption of new ideas is not automatic. Constant communication, motivation, and problem solving move the adoption process forward and combat the constant gravitational pull back to the status quo. Implementing a new business strategy is like paddling upstream against the current of the status quo—if you stop paddling, you will drift back to where you came from. Implementation and change-management efforts must be constant until the new business approach becomes the new norm.

As I mentioned earlier, leading the implementation of any business change, big or small, in an organization can be a complicated endeavor. The best business strategies and plans can fizzle during implementation if not orchestrated and managed effectively. Managing change is not a matter of giving orders and expecting "the troops" to follow commands. Rather, it is a complicated mixture of strategy, planning, management, and psychology.

Consider an overly simplified example of a process change in a small work group. An inexperienced manager might understand the outcome that a process is expected to produce. The eager inexperienced manager might charge ahead and make the required changes with little regard for the consequences to the people involved. This inexperienced manager might start by announcing the required changes to the employees, which may include changes to work flow, tasks, responsibilities, or job assignments. The inexperienced manager might overlook unknown skill requirements, group dynamics, or other consequences that may impact the people involved.

Most managers with even a little experience would more likely explain to the employees why a change is necessary, what change is going to be made, and the overall expectations, as well as outline the actual work flow, answer questions, and seek feedback on potential problems. In this oversimplified example, the change seems fairly straightforward and uncomplicated. However, in reality, digesting a change, large or small, can be extremely complicated and disruptive and can inspire organized resistance to the new business approach. A carefully planned and executed approach can result in an effective, swift, and successful implementation of the new business initiative. It can develop active promoters and increase the number of early adopters. The right preparation and ingredients can actually accelerate the implementation without unduly increasing the risk of failure. After witnessing a couple of decades' worth of good and poor examples, I developed the Accelerated Implementation Model for this exact purpose.

The Accelerated Implementation Model has five major topic areas:

1. Acceleration Prerequisites

2. An Accelerator's Tool Kit

3. Methodically Grow Active Support

4. Attentively Manage the Implementation

5. Embed the New Business Strategy

The book follows this process flow and provides practical tips from experience along the way. First, let's have a look at the Accelerated Implementation Model.

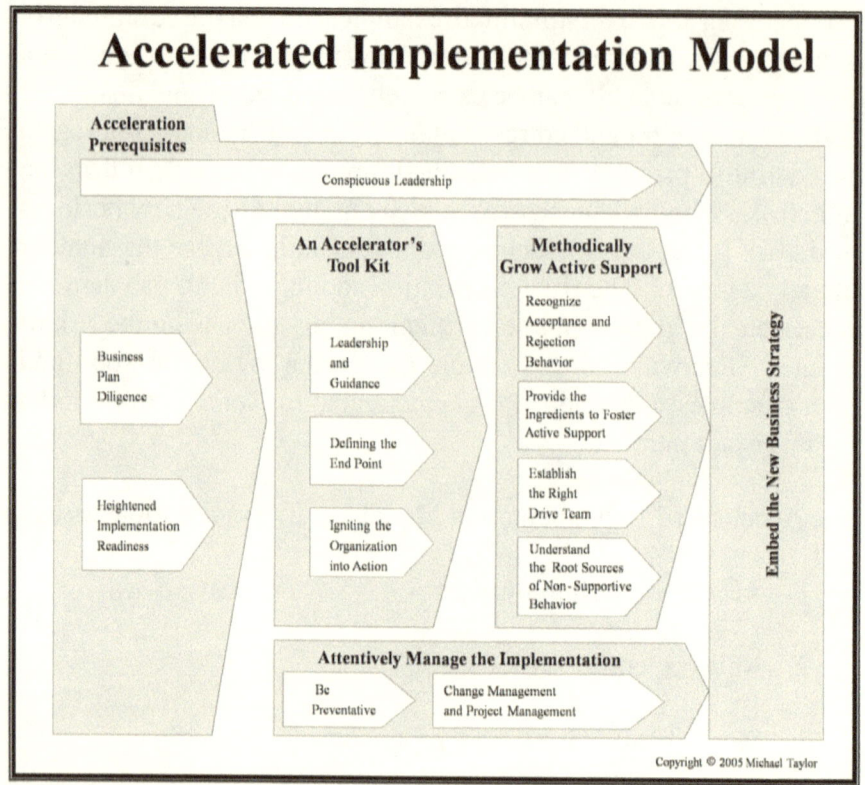

Acceleration Prerequisites

There are many important elements of success, but there are a few that are critical prerequisites if you are planning to accelerate the implementation of new business initiatives. These critical prerequisites include the following:

- Conspicuous leadership: guidance and motivation that is overt and exhibited. Conspicuous involvement of the whole leadership team. Articulation of where we are going and the benefits of the new business approach and encouraging people to safely and confidently adopt the approaches outlined in the new business strategy.

- A rock-solid business strategy, including business plans grounded in confirmed facts and research. Is this new initiative worth the risk and cost of making changes?

- Preparedness, a heightened implementation readiness and an understanding of the expected impact or disruption to normal operations. The placement of experienced people to lead the implementation, the alignment of the senior management team, and a heightened state of readiness throughout the organization.

These elements, or ingredients, of prelaunch are a sample of the core prerequisites before implementation. The following chapters will provide explanations and tips from experience on these prerequisites.

An Accelerator's Tool Kit

An accelerated strategy implementation requires the organization to quickly understand and accept new ideas and then aggressively engage in the implementation. This does not happen automatically.

As we will discuss in later chapters, the process of growing from acceptance to engaged support takes time and effort. However, there are some tools we can prepare that will help people in the organization with the adoption process—ultimately accelerating adoption and implementation. This portion of the process includes a discussion of the role of leadership and a description of several of the accelerator's tools, such as the "Compelling Attraction" and the "100-Second Enlightenment."

We all know that leadership is much more than management. Leading a business change such as the implementation of a new business strategy amplifies the need for organizational leadership. In particular, during the introduction of the new business strategy, the organization needs three elements:

- Leadership and guidance: guidance to explain the new business strategy, the expected outcome, and why the new plan is better than the existing situation as well as to unite the organization to implement the new strategy. Leadership to empower culture change, and generate confidence that the new approach will be successful.

- A defined end point and a Compelling Attraction to clarify and synchronize what everyone is working toward and to motivate the organization, and a 100-Second Enlightenment, a synopsis that pulls the message all together.

- An Igniting Event to spark the organization into action and synchronize their efforts onto one action plan.

Methodically Grow Active Support

Growing strong support is the foundation of implementing any new idea. As the title of this section implies, support is not instantaneous—you must grow support. However, we want more than passive support. To accelerate the implementation of a new strategy, we need active support. In the following chapters, we will discuss the process of methodically growing active support as a means to accelerate business-strategy implementation.

People do not switch from their current norms to a new business strategy instantaneously. Most people go through a process that starts with accepting the fact that the status quo is unacceptable and ends with varying degrees of support. Support can vary from those who are strong advocates of the new plan and who help drive accelerated adoption to those who are entrenched opponents of the new plan and recruit cohorts. During the adoption process, each individual goes through his or her own individual stages of acceptance and/or rejection. Each individual adopts or rebuffs at his or her own rate. The successful leader who wants to accelerate the implementation of a new initiative recognizes that people differ, understands the acceptance process, and enacts the best ingredients, talent, and tools to win acceptance and generate active support—the phases of the adoption/rejection process. The process is a series of steps, of gradual understanding and acceptance. Reluctance or anxiety in the organization can diminish or evaporate support and delay your business implementation. It is important not to lose sight of the adoption process and to assist people through it. In the following chapters, we explore the elements to methodically grow active support:

- recognize acceptance and rejection behavior

- provide the ingredients to foster active support

- establish the right drive team

- understand the root sources of non-supportive behavior

Attentively Manage the Implementation

Once the new business initiative is defined, many managers feel a need to dive into planning the implementation while overlooking many of the preparatory elements outlined above. Experienced managers, remembering the implementation difficulties they have witnessed throughout their careers, naturally apply their experience to define an implementation plan that benefits from that experience—but they still often focus on the implementation and overlook the preparation. We will spend much of this book discussing preparation and preventative measures that can make the implementation go more smoothly and faster. Even though preparation is a key element of accelerated strategy implementation, attentively managing the implementation of your new strategy is equally critical to accelerated success. We will discuss practical approaches, provide tips to help make implementation plans more effective, and outline common pitfalls that can unnecessarily delay success. The points outlined in this section are not from any theory or ideology. As you will see, these tips are from experience.

Embed the New Business Strategy

The conclusion of the new strategy implementation is a time of conflicting needs. We need to rest from the high-effort implementation activity while becoming comfortable with new business practices. We sometimes foresee the end of the implementation as "task accomplished" and a time to rest. Usually the opposite is true—there is pressure to aggressively take advantage of the changes and perhaps to take advantage of new market opportunities or to catch competition before any more ground is lost. Nevertheless, people need to sense and experience some stability and now become comfortable with new approaches, new work environments, new processes, or maybe new jobs. This is not a time to rest, but it is a time to stabilize with no further changes. The "new" business strategy needs to become "our" business strategy. Once the implementation is complete, the organization needs to get into a mind-set of stabilization, reduced anxiety, and the normal turmoil of daily business. The organization needs to get back on a path of high productivity and deliver the business performance expected from the new business initiative. In this part of the Accelerated Implementation Model, we share some ideas from experience to help embed the new business strategy, make it stick, and transition from "implementing the new strategy" to "normal operating mode."

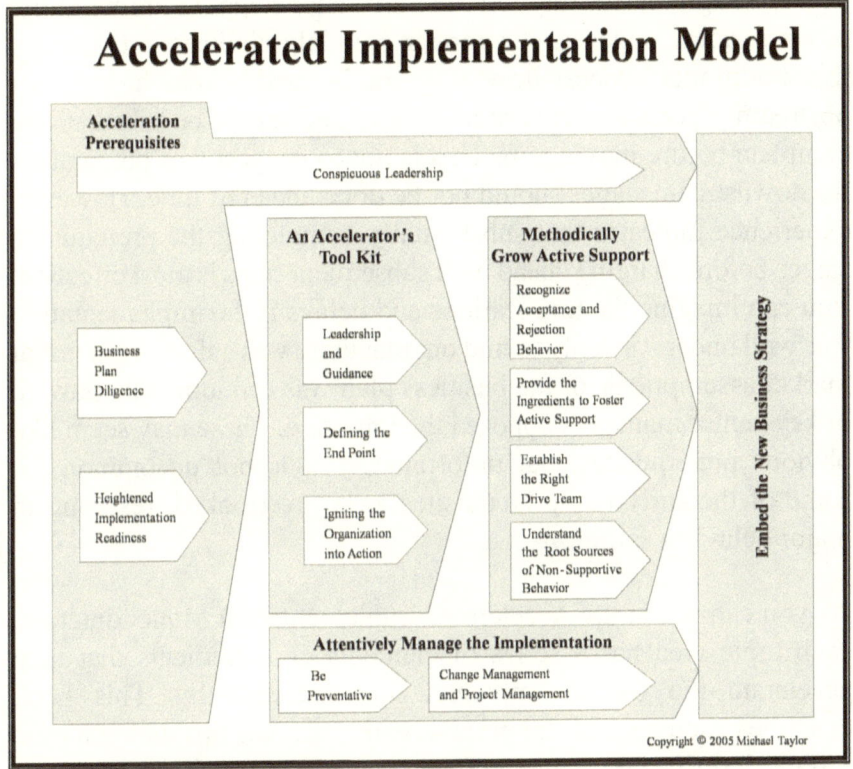

The Accelerated Implementation Model is a "prerequisite contributory" process. That is, the elements early in the process are required essentials (prerequisites) for later elements to build upon (contribute to). An example may make this easier to explain. As with most aspects of management, a fundamental ingredient is leadership. However, leadership can only contribute to the success of a sound "business strategy and plan." Alone, "leadership" will not drive business results. Likewise, "change management" and "project management" contribute to the prerequisite leadership elements. Without the leadership elements in place, all that follows will be much less effective. Without the right ingredients substantially in place, your new initiative, even if it is the greatest business plan of all time, could severely disrupt an otherwise functioning organization.

The process elements are displayed in the Accelerated Implementation Model diagram, starting on the left and stepping through the process. Some stages can be done in parallel as indicated. However, this traditional process-flow diagram is used to emphasize that upstream process steps are prerequisites and should be substantially complete before moving on. This is not to suggest that preparation for downstream stages should not be done ahead of time. However, experience indicates that substantially completing the prerequisite stages before charging ahead with subsequent steps is most effective. You can imagine the implications and delays if the implementation was well under way only to find out that there was a flaw in the initial market assumptions, or the business plan was economically flawed, or key senior managers opposed the initiative. These may seem like obvious prerequisites, but unfortunately it is not uncommon for some of the early key prerequisites to be overlooked, resulting in major delays or failure.

As you can see in the Accelerated Implementation Model diagram, each topic area has a series of elements or ingredients that help accelerate the overall implementation successfully. This book describes each area of the process with practical tips and common pitfalls described throughout. The explanation of each area serves to illustrate the ingredients that help accelerate the implementation of new business initiatives or new business strategies. It is beneficial to read the chapters in order. Some of the most common problems result from missing prerequisites or from weak ingredients that play a key part in success. Like any fine recipe, every ingredient is important.

The Accelerated Implementation Model will make it easier to paddle upstream against the status quo and easier to embed the new norm quickly.

Part I

Acceleration Prerequisites

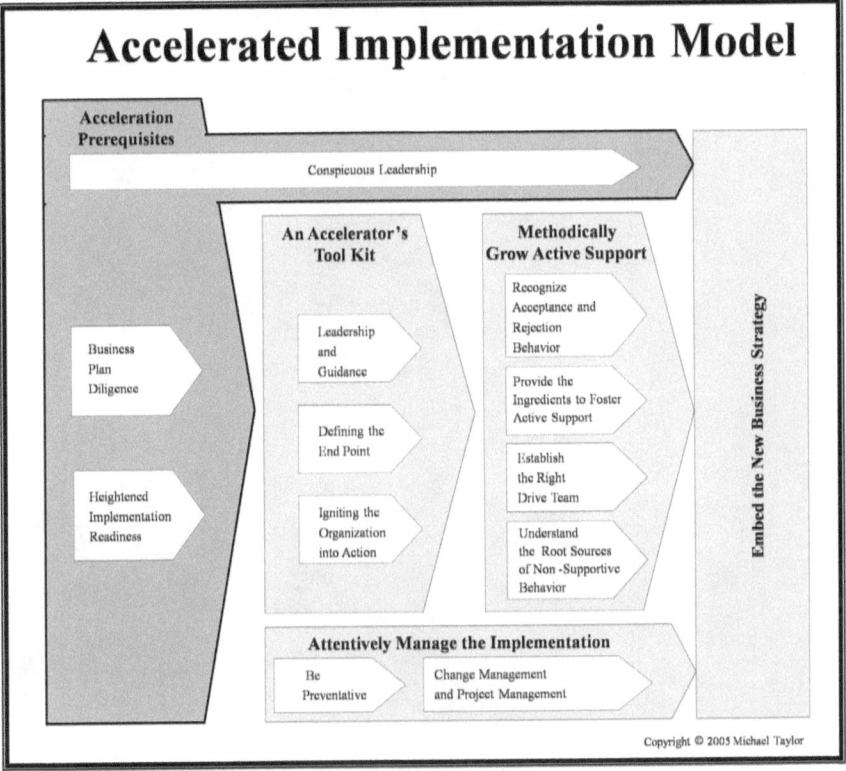

Accelerated Implementation Model

Acceleration Prerequisites

Conspicuous Leadership

Business Plan Diligence

Heightened Implementation Readiness

An Accelerator's Tool Kit

Leadership and Guidance

Defining the End Point

Igniting the Organization into Action

Methodically Grow Active Support

Recognize Acceptance and Rejection Behavior

Provide the Ingredients to Foster Active Support

Establish the Right Drive Team

Understand the Root Sources of Non-Supportive Behavior

Attentively Manage the Implementation

Be Preventative

Change Management and Project Management

Embed the New Business Strategy

Copyright © 2005 Michael Taylor

1

Introduction

There are many important elements of success, but there are a few that are critical prerequisites if you are planning to accelerate the implementation of new business initiatives. There are three critical prerequisites:

- Conspicuous leadership. Exhibited guidance and motivation of the leadership team, articulating where we are going and the benefits of the new business approach and encouraging people to safely and confidently adopt the approaches outlined in the new business strategy.

- A rock-solid business strategy, including business plans grounded in confirmed facts and research.

- Preparedness, a heightened implementation readiness and an understanding of the expected impact or disruption to normal operations. The placement of experienced people to lead the implementation and the alignment of the senior management team behind the new initiative as key steps in heightened readiness.

These elements of prelaunch are core prerequisites before implementation. In this section we will explore the crucial prerequisites and share some tips from experience.

Chapter 1

Conspicuous Leadership

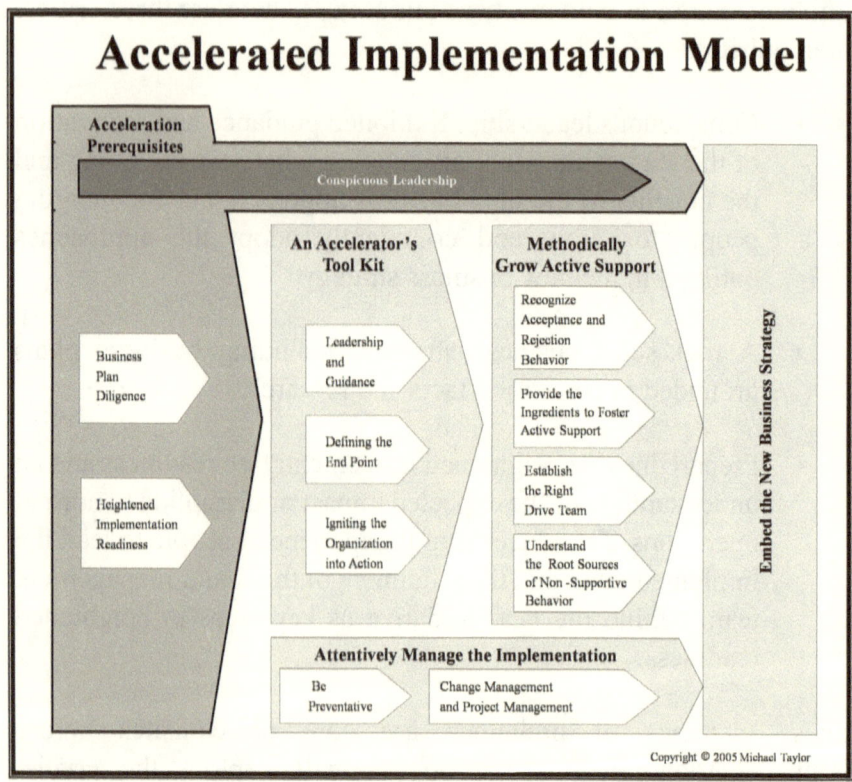

Accelerated Implementation Model

Acceleration Prerequisites

Conspicuous Leadership

An Accelerator's Tool Kit

Methodically Grow Active Support

Business Plan Diligence

Leadership and Guidance

Recognize Acceptance and Rejection Behavior

Provide the Ingredients to Foster Active Support

Defining the End Point

Establish the Right Drive Team

Heightened Implementation Readiness

Igniting the Organization into Action

Understand the Root Sources of Non-Supportive Behavior

Embed the New Business Strategy

Attentively Manage the Implementation

Be Preventative

Change Management and Project Management

Leadership, Not Just the Leader

It should be no surprise that a critical element of the accelerated implementation process begins with leadership. I use the term "leadership" and not "leader," because people in the organization view a broad range of the management team as the leadership. During the implementation of a major corporate strategy, the leadership will usually be perceived as all executives in the company. On the other hand, when implementing a new business strategy in a smaller firm or the local operations of a major firm, the leadership is likely to be perceived as the senior manager or owner and the small group of people who play a large part in leading the operations of the organization.

The energy diverted to implementing the new business plan and consequently the speed of adoption is generally higher when the organization perceives that the whole leadership team is driving the new plan. If the new strategy seems to be the endeavor of one person, even if that person is the CEO, the project will not generate as much enthusiasm or support—it may be perceived simply as "the project of the month." We all know the key role of the implementation leader during the planning and implementation stage of a new business initiative. However, the organization needs to know that the management leadership team is driving the change. If the implementation leader is the lone management voice promoting the new initiative, it can quite easily be viewed as a minor program and have difficulty garnering the level of support that comes with the active support of the management leadership team. Broad leadership support is the first prerequisite in the process, because without it the new business plan will have difficulty getting any initial inertia.

As we will see in later chapters, the speed of adoption in the organization is greatly increased if they

- understand the strategy and why the change is necessary,

- know that the leadership supports the new strategy (ideally with top-to-bottom leadership support, although this is difficult to achieve on day one in large organizations), and

- most importantly, have confidence in the leadership's ability to be successful.

Develop Leadership Support First

It is hard for the leadership team to provide credibility to the new strategy and develop confidence in success if they are not informed and convinced that the new strategy is the best course of action.

Time invested in developing broad and deep leadership support will give an early boost to the adoption speed of the new business plan and provide a stronger platform to accelerate the new strategy implementation.

Be Conspicuous

The word "Conspicuous" in the chapter title is very intentional. The phrase "out front" would be equally as appropriate. The support, guidance, and motivation of the leadership team must be blatantly obvious to the people in the organization. Hearing the details of the plan, the reasons behind the plan, and the benefits of the plan directly from members of the leadership team builds confidence and consequently faster and more pervasive adoption of the new business strategy. Direct communications from the leadership allow people in the organization to get more than the literal meaning in the message. They can sense the enthusiasm and the confidence the leadership has in the new strategy. The importance of the new strategy is reinforced when the people in the organization see the effort and emphasis being put on the new strategy directly by the leadership team. This not only demonstrates the importance of the new strategy but builds confidence in the management team and credibility for the new business plan. Conspicuous leadership usually means increased direct contact with people throughout the organization. As a side benefit, this can also provide opportunities for employees to ask questions and get immediate replies to their questions. They can hear the sincerity and commitment in the responses from the leadership team.

Conspicuous leadership is not just a kickoff activity. If the people in the organization see the leadership commitment only at the kickoff of the new business strategy, there is a stronger likelihood that the new business strategy will be perceived as "the project of the month" and not generate a sustained effort to implement the new business initiatives. A sustained effort by the leadership team to conspicuously demonstrate their commitment to the new business strategy will grow a stronger base of sustained support throughout the organization.

Chapter 2

Diligent Business Plan Review

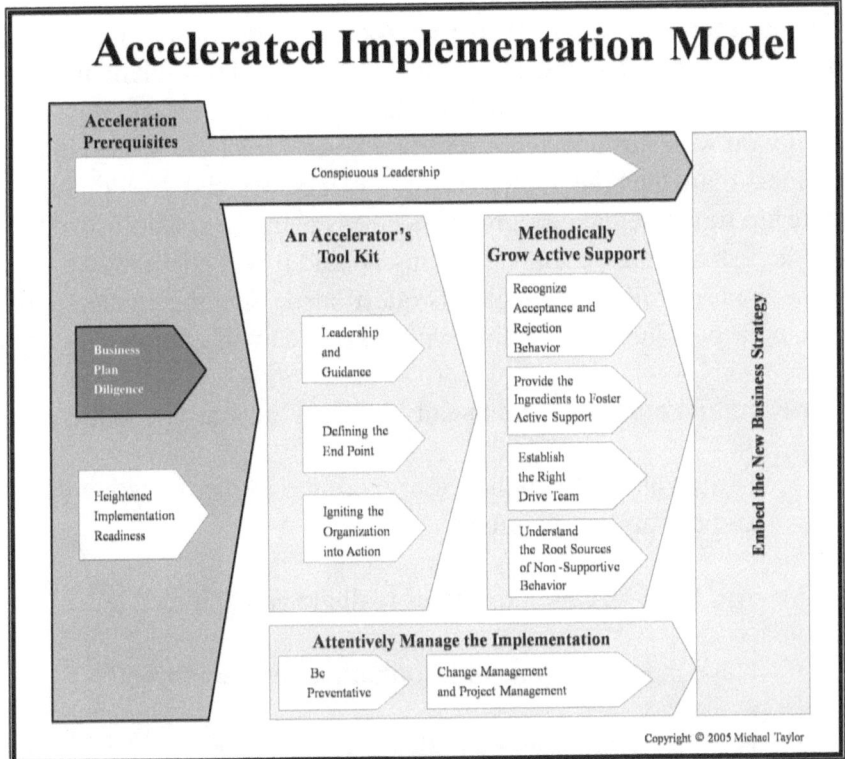

Accelerated Implementation Model

Acceleration Prerequisites

Conspicuous Leadership

An Accelerator's Tool Kit

Methodically Grow Active Support

Business Plan Diligence

Leadership and Guidance

Recognize Acceptance and Rejection Behavior

Provide the Ingredients to Foster Active Support

Defining the End Point

Establish the Right Drive Team

Heightened Implementation Readiness

Igniting the Organization into Action

Understand the Root Sources of Non-Supportive Behavior

Embed the New Business Strategy

Attentively Manage the Implementation

Be Preventative

Change Management and Project Management

Copyright © 2005 Michael Taylor

Why Review the Plan? After All, We Just Created It

It is prudent to conduct a diligent review of the business plan before you get started with an accelerated implementation of the new business strategy. In all likelihood, the ink on the business strategy is not dry and the details of the business plan are still being worked out while people start to organize the implementation. In the excitement, or panic, to get going, omissions or mistakes can easily be made, conclusions can be hasty, and assumptions can be left unconfirmed. It is advantageous to make an objective and diligent review of the business strategy and plan before commencing. This

7

is the point for a sanity check. Upon reflection, is this new strategy really the right move? Can you really make the benefits materialize? Do the merits outweigh the costs? Can you mobilize the resources and organizational support fast enough to make it pay off?

Making modifications to the plan is easier and much faster before you leave the starting gate than after. Avoid the trap of solely thinking strategically and leaving the tactical details to the implementation team. If the implementation team has to spend a lot of time and energy on work-around activities to make up for shortcomings in the business plan, then the implementation will be delayed. In addition, if there are fundamental flaws in the business plan, the credibility of the whole plan and all the sound thinking behind it will come into doubt. Once the credibility of the plan is questioned, then the challenge of gaining acceptance and dealing with resistance will compound.

There are five questions that usually will put the strategy to the test:

- Is the change really necessary; are the implementation costs and disruption justified?

- Are the goals and objectives realistic and achievable?

- Have the critical bits of information been confirmed?

- Have the risks been identified and mitigated?

- Have the implementation expectations, timelines, and costs been defined?

Let's explore each of these points a little more.

Is Change Really Necessary?

The first question is "What is wrong with the status quo?" If we consider the implementation costs and disruption costs of the new business strategy, maybe a minor modification to the existing situation can achieve the same bottom-line result.

In business, we are always looking for the optimum approach, and it is sometimes easy to allow the benefits of a new strategy to overshadow the costs associated with making the change to the new strategy. The implementation cost as well as the cost associated with disruption of the current business can be significant and is sometimes overlooked.

Don't fall into the trap of implementing a new strategy or a major initiative simply to allow a new leader (maybe it's you) to put their (your) personal stamp on the organization. We all have recollections of leaders who have a need to demonstrate that they are having an impact and making a visible change. It is easy to look at unconfirmed benefits of a new initiative and neglect the associated costs.

Sometimes the best way to confirm that this is the right decision is to start to build a business case to justify the new strategy. The business case should be written with two audiences in mind: board members and shop-floor (or frontline) employees. These two perspectives will force you to think strategically and tactically, long term and short term, about overall business benefits and shop-floor changes, enterprise-wide implementation requirements and business-disruption costs. The business case you prepare will have another use as well. It can be used as part of the messaging plan to gain acceptance from the people impacted. As you ask affected employees to adopt and implement the initiatives associated with the new business strategy, the first challenge will be to gain their acceptance. Those employees who are directly affected will be among the first required to accept the need for change over the easy path of the status quo.

The business case should answer some key questions: Why are we doing this? What do we plan to do? Is it worth it?

The business case should address these points:

- What are the factors driving the need for change?

- Why is this new strategy or initiative necessary?

- Why we need to implement this now? What is the urgency?

- What are the options?

- Why is the chosen alternative best?

- A description of the strategy.

- A summary of the strategic benefits (e.g., market positioning) of the new strategy.

- A summary of the projected value of the benefits.

- A list of the business areas expected to be most impacted by the new strategy.

- A summary of the expected changes required to implement the new strategy.

- A summary of the expected disruption, implementation costs, and timeline.

- A summary of the parameters that will measure success or completion.

It may be prudent to bring in someone with a fresh new perspective to review the plan and perhaps identify pitfalls that remain hidden to those who are reviewing their own work. The answer to the question "Why is change necessary?" should be in plain language that can be communicated to all the stakeholders in the organization. The business case should be detailed enough for senior managers to see the integrity in the plan and be explained in a straightforward way that is easy enough for employees who are not deeply involved in managing the company to understand the explanations.

I was asked to join a task force a number of years ago. The team was given the assignment of planning the integration of several support groups from different divisions of a large company. The goal was to integrate the various groups into one that would support various divisions. Each individual group had a similar supporting role in their respective division. Strategically, it made sense. Strategically, we could list a series of benefits. However, a closer examination revealed the strong interdependencies that each group had with other parts of their respective divisions. Although there were benefits to integrating the various groups, the counterbalancing costs associated with supporting the divisions from a central support group outweighed the benefits. After a diligent review of this initiative, it was discovered that the new idea was not worth the cost. The integration did not go forward.

Realistic and Achievable Objectives

Are the goals and objectives of the new initiatives realistic and achievable? There is a time and a place for stretch targets. Implementing a new business strategy or major corporate initiative causes a great deal of turmoil during the implementation. It is challenging enough to accelerate the implementation. This is not the time for stretch goals.

Setting objectives for the implementation of a new business strategy is different from setting normal operating objectives. In normal operating conditions, there is merit in setting stretch targets. However, major change will always invoke some degree of skepticism, which may make stretch targets seem like an unattainable ambition. In a major change situation, stretch targets may dishearten your people rather than inspire them to reach higher. Remember that much of a typical population does not eagerly embrace change. The first challenge will be the acceptance of the need for change. The second challenge is the acceptance of the new business model. Setting attainable goals will make it easier for the majority of the population to feel confident that the new plan will be successful. Faster widespread acceptance accelerates adoption. The majority of the organization should view change-management goals as achievable. In times where drastic change is needed, it is best to outline the overall objective and then specifically point out the short-term attainable goals to help your people see the attainable steps to reach the overall objective—perhaps goals for various phases or various business groups or various functional areas.

Realistic and attainable goals will give you the benefit of the doubt in the early "buy-in" period and help develop credibility and support for the new plan. This will start to generate the early inertia necessary to get started.

Confirmation of the Critical Bits

Although it may seem obvious, it still needs to be said: your business plan should be founded on confirmed facts. The situation analysis is usually based on market, competitive, and operating information that has driven certain conclusions. Usually this is a combination of firsthand hard facts, information from secondary sources, assessments based on observations, and assumptions. Often, however, there are a few key pieces of information that are driving the need for change, your strategy, and your business plans.

Be diligent. Review and distill your analysis so you reveal and understand the "critical bits" of information that you are building your plans on. Double-check and confirm the "critical bits" of information and the "critical bits" of analysis to make sure your plan is on a solid foundation. Not every fact or conclusion needs to be confirmed and verified by multiple sources, but the "critical bits" need to be airtight.

During the rollout of the new strategy or initiative, it is amazing how quickly employees who know the business very well can hone in on a critical flaw in a piece of information and discredit the plan in front of their peers. Demonstrating that the new business approach is based on sound information and research is a key part of accelerating the employee acceptance of the new business plan and ultimately accelerating the implementation of the overall strategy.

It is dangerous to overlook this step, because a conclusion based on wrong data can nullify the benefits of the strategy or lead to a wrong course of action that cannot be corrected by simply altering the rollout plan later.

Risks and Mitigation

What business review would be complete without looking at risks? Implementing a new business strategy is no different. If you want to accelerate your business-strategy implementation, you need to look at the risks associated with this type of change management. This section is not intended to be a comprehensive review of business risk but rather a focus on the risks associated with the accelerated implementation of business initiatives and the consequent changes. After this review, it may be decided that an alternative strategy with lower risk is actually the optimal course of action.

Accelerating business plan implementation does not mean blindly charging ahead at full speed without consideration of risk. A prelaunch risk review is one of the most prudent accelerators there is. Risk is inevitable. The key is to identify and mitigate the critical risks and be prepared to quickly solve other problems to avoid delays.

The risk review could ask questions of the strategy and the strategy implementation.

Sample strategy risk questions:

- Why did we select this strategy? What was the evaluation process? Has a sober objective review been completed?

- How attainable are the potential merits and benefits?

- How material are the threats to the existing situation?

- How realistic are the numbers in the business case? Have we had an experienced eye review the estimates?

- How abundant are the resources required? Are there any sourcing bottlenecks or risks associated with potential supply limits?

- Can we mobilize fast enough to take advantage of the opportunity benefits? What are the consequences if we are late?

- Is there any unproven technology or technology integration risks? What are the consequences if it doesn't work right the first time—failure or delay?

Sample implementation risk questions:

- Can the implementation leader meet the timeline and objectives?

- Have key resources and people been confirmed? How will the loss of key people impact the implementation?

- What will be the impact of any leadership commitments that do not materialize?

- Will there be enough time for the extra work required to carry out implementation activities?

- What will be the impact if the disruption to ongoing business has been underestimated?

- At what point are we committed and cannot return to the old system?

- Where are the most likely cost overruns to occur?

For each identified risk, there is an obvious supplementary question. What steps can we take to avoid the potential problem or prepare for it to minimize the impact of such a risk? In addition, there are countless tactical risks that accompany any rollout. We cannot prepare for every inevitable consequence without getting bogged down to a halt. To accelerate business-strategy implementation, we need to prepare for the inevitable problems, obstacles, and issues. The best way to minimize the impact of problems along the way is to solve them quickly. Here are four tips to help:

1. Have a "problem resolution" system, contact person, or hot line for management and employees to call with questions so issues can become visible right away.

2. Welcome feedback and expect problems. Don't treat them as criticism, complaining, or roadblocks.

3. Predefine decision-authority limits and empower the implementation team with as much authority as possible to solve issues quickly. It is often hard to define this authority in the beginning. As the implementation is under way, encourage the implementation team to solve problems themselves. When they come to the senior team with issues, inform them which ones you would prefer to have settled by the team themselves. This way the team's authority level is quickly defined. Also, the detailed description in the "Compelling Attraction," which we will discuss in a later chapter, will help the implementation team make decisions that are aligned with the prescribed end result. This allows the decision team to make decisions that are aligned with this detailed vision and limits escalation issues to real problems and not just clarifications.

4. Predetermine the escalation path and the expectations of availability and response time of executives in the escalation path.

Implementation problems and challenges always occur. A key element of accelerating the business-strategy implementation is to prepare to solve problems quickly and minimize their impact.

Implementation Expectations, Timelines, and Costs

There are key questions that need to be asked here: How will we know when the plan is implemented? What defines completion? How will we measure that success? It may seem obvious that a business plan review includes a review of the implementation expectations, the progress and completion deadlines, and the cost associated with the resources required. Even though it may seem obvious, this is sometimes the first time everyone on the senior management team really understands what specifically they will have to change or commit to, what people will be allocated to the implementation team, and the total cost associated with the implementation.

This is the time when the implementation leader gets to really understand the performance expectations being asked of him or her. The only way you can avoid scope creep and scapegoatism is to have a well-defined definition of implementation completion. The implementation leader's next steps are to make sure the objectives can be accomplished within the budget and resources available and to define the frequency and type of progress reporting required.

This is the time when the business plan requirements become tangible enough to surface any lingering confusion or resistance in the senior team. The acid test of support for each senior manager is their commitment of budget, people, and their own time. It is valuable to get each senior manager's commitment to an action plan . including communication commitments.

There are a few key elements of the time line and expectations review:

- Describe the factors that define completion.

- Define the milestone delivery dates of key stages or deliverables.

- Define the budget amount, any limitations on the types of expenditures to be funded, and the approval process to make spending commitments.

- Get agreement from senior management on their required action plans.

- Get agreement from senior management on people in their organization who will be assigned (not necessarily full-time) to support the implementation plan.

- Define the frequency and format of the progress reports the senior management will require from the implementation leader.

Chapter 3

Heightened Implementation Readiness

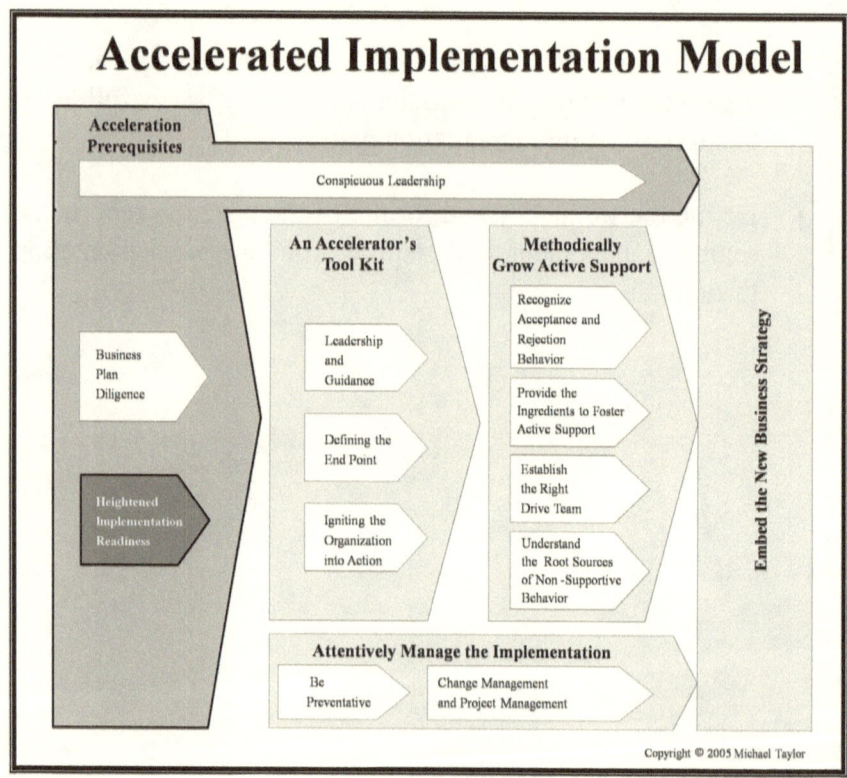

The Importance of Readiness

The greatest business strategy in the world can fall flat if it is not well implemented. Strategy execution starts long before the formal announcement. Preannouncement preparedness can make the difference between an enthusiastic and inspiring kickoff and a fizzled dud on the starting line. Preparing for the launch of the new business strategy is critical and involves a lot more than drafting the rollout announcement. As soon as the new strategy is announced, a number of reactions typically occur.

1. People in the organization will interpret the consequences of the announcement and the impact the new business plan will have on them personally. They will almost immediately entrench their favorable or unfavorable opinion of the change.

2. People in the organization will each interpret the end result of the new business strategy based on their own individual knowledge and past experience, which means that almost every person will envision a different end result.

3. Small-group discussions about the implications of the new business strategy will cause distraction from normal business. In extreme cases, this can distract some people to idleness, can transform top-performing employees into disgruntled saboteurs, can ball up infrastructure systems with inquiries, and can grind productivity to a halt.

4. Some people will eagerly support the new plan and help lead the change.

These typical reactions are not limited to frontline employees—they reach into the most senior levels of management as well.

With this knowledge in mind, it is important to prepare for the reactions we expect. If we want an accelerated implementation, then a key success factor is early support from as many people as possible, especially the senior management team. To start with, we need one common interpretation of the new business strategy. There are a number of steps that can be taken before the business strategy is announced to foster support and accelerate implementation.

Here are some key preparation elements:

- Explain the plan and gain the support of the senior management team, especially the leaders of any mission-critical groups.

- Prepare the senior team for the expected organizational behavior patterns and resistance that are typical during the implementation period of a new business initiative.

- Appoint an experienced implementation leader and explain his or her responsibilities to the senior team.

- Develop a messaging plan to ensure that the entire senior team and all subsequent communications deliver a consistent message and a consistent explanation of the message.

- Define the implementation plan and expectations—rollout approach, expected progress, results, and timelines—and construct a measurement-and-reward system to manage the implementation progress.

Adoption of most major changes like a new business strategy usually starts with a core group of leaders and systematically spreads through the organization. The preparation to strengthen the core group at the beginning is a big step toward heightening the organization's implementation readiness. Ultimately the payoff for this effort in the beginning will be increased confidence in the management team, reduced anxiety in the organization, an accelerated adoption rate, and a smoother transition.

Senior Management and Mission-Critical Groups

As part of the readiness strategy, it is important to have the senior management team in full support of the plan. Identify and defuse any suspected senior management resistance. As the new business strategy is unfolded, the organization will quickly sense divisions in the senior team that will undermine the credibility of the business strategy and slow adoption. Senior management blockades can easily arise when the old guard is being pushed aside or portions of the organization are losing influence or when senior executives disagree on the new strategy. If key senior people are not in full support of the new initiative, then you are not ready for kickoff announcements. Resistance at this level will only be amplified in the organization.

Major changes often have an impact on a wide number of groups, departments, divisions, or business units. However, in most cases there are segments of the organization that will play a critical role in the success of the new strategy. It is important to gain the early support of the leadership of these mission-critical groups. This core-team senior executives and mission-critical leaders must be ready to actively support the plan in front of their employees. By paying more than just lip service, their method of operating and their actions must visibly be in full support of the new strategy.

In the early stages of preparation, there is usually a desire to keep news of the new business strategy limited to a rather small group until all the alternatives are evaluated and the strategy is solidified. Nevertheless it is often beneficial to gain input from mission-critical groups so that some of the practical and tactical aspects of the new plan can be fine-tuned and perhaps to secure early support from the leaders of mission-critical groups. This inclusion of mission-critical groups for early fine-tuning can provide a key advantage to accelerating the business-strategy implementation. It is always a judgment call as to how many people to include beyond the senior team to secure this support. The more people are involved, the more likely you are to have information leaks and fuel rumors before your communication plan is launched.

The purpose of garnering the early support of the senior team and the leaders of mission-critical groups is to set the stage for this group to deliver a consistent supportive message regarding the business change. This bolsters confidence in the organization, which in turn sets the stage for accelerated adoption of the new strategy in the critical early days after the launch announcement. Going forward, the role of the core executive team will be more than just to act as a managing board or steering committee. When driving a new business strategy, these powerful and influential people need to actively promote the merits of the new business plan, provide support and advice to any implementation teams, mobilize resources, reallocate budgets, and when required, intervene to diffuse resistance with mid-level managers in their respective organizations.

Prepare for the Expected Organizational Behavior and Resistance

The execution of a new business strategy is normally intended to drive some type of change into the business and ultimately increase performance. Often the senior management's focus is on the strategy and expected performance improvement, leaving the part in the middle—the prescribed change to the business—with less attention than it needs. It is this middle part—the changes to business operations and practices—that will drive the resulting behavior of the people in the organization. Heightening implementation readiness includes preparing the management team for the expected organizational behavior and resistance during and after implementation.

Not every new business initiative is a major divergence from the past. A new business strategy can have modest impact on the organization or, at the other extreme, drive a complicated set of leadership, organizational, process, functional, and systems' changes. As part of implementation readiness, the senior management team not only needs to understand the business-system changes but to understand the complex behavior patterns that the new strategy is likely to drive in the organization.

Implementation readiness means helping the management team and the leaders of the affected groups understand what to expect. Not just the new systems, the new processes, and the new organizational report lines, but also the psychological impact on the people in the organization, the normal resistive feelings, the extra communication required, what groups may balk because they are losing political power in the organization, and so on. We will cover many of these topics later in this book. To accelerate the new strategy implementation, it is helpful for the management team to consider and plan for the expected behavior of people in the organization. This will allow the management team to formulate their communication messages to help reduce anxiety, diffuse potential resistance, and resolve problems more quickly—all contributing factors to expedited adoption and accelerated implementation.

The actions of the senior team will have a large impact on the accelerated adoption of the new business plan activities. When the organization's leaders are addressing or interacting with people in the organization, their words and actions are always being interpreted. Most senior executives are accustomed to this and carry themselves professionally. With a heightened insight into the expected organizational behavior and resistance involved during a business change, your executive leaders can take advantage of opportunities to reduce anxiety and accelerate adoption and avoid inadvertently creating resistance. The most dangerous times are during unscripted responses to employee questions. Without a good understanding of expected organizational behavior during a major change, executives are at a leadership disadvantage. We will explore this more in the section on understanding resistance later in the book.

It is valuable to have a prelaunch briefing session with the senior team so the team can discuss the behavior that they expect will result after the announcement of the new business strategy. The magnitude of the prescribed business change and the experience of the senior team will define the appropriate level of briefing required. It may suffice to have a discussion of the expected organization behavior at a normal executive meeting. Alternatively, you may decide that an executive briefing with an experienced professional in the field is in order.

You may think some of this is overreacting. However, from my experience, I can state: "Don't expect to find change management skills as part of the standard skill set in the organization (shop floor to senior management). Most managers are managers, not leaders (strike 1). Most managers have little experience operating in the unstructured or abstract environment of a major change (strike 2). Most managers have little experience operating in an environment where they must drive change through parts of the organization that they do not have direct control over—influence and no power (strike 3)."

The senior team has a role to coach many of the mid-level managers. During the turmoil of implementing any major change, the senior team balances the desire to accelerate the implementation with the patience required to allow mid-level managers to effectively adopt the new ideas, new systems, and new processes, all the while keeping the business operating. A fresh appreciation for the behavioral issues created during major change will improve the senior team's effectiveness during this critical time and contribute to accelerated adoption of the new business strategy.

Appoint the Right Implementation Leader

As you read through this book and start to think about the impact your new business strategy will have on the organization, the changes required, and the organizational behavior expected, you will begin to see the level of management required to successfully accelerate the implementation of a new business strategy or corporate initiative (major or minor). With this understanding, you have taken a major step in your readiness for an accelerated strategy implementation. You will likely start to foresee the complexity, the management efforts, and the resources required during the implementation phase—and this is where the implementation leader enters the scene.

Think about the magnitude of change required to move from the existing situation to the model defined in the new strategy. This will give some indication of the amount of leadership attention required. You can consider whether one of the senior managers in the organization can be the implementation leader while maintaining their current responsibilities or if this assignment needs the full-time attention of someone during the implementation period. Regardless of whether the implementation leader is a full-time responsibility or not, it is important to assign this accountability and communicate the responsibility to the executive team so they can include this in their communications and provide the implementation leader with the necessary support.

The right implementation leader can have more impact than anyone else on the speed, effectiveness, and success of the rollout of the new plan. Experience in the business area is an asset, but experience in successfully leading other similar implementations and familiarity with change-management challenges should be the priority when selecting a change leader. This is not project management. There is also a need for project management—making sure all the details are looked after, all the interdependent activities are synchronized, all the resources are in the right place at the right time, and that the overall plan stays on schedule to meet deadlines. However, project management and change management are not the same. The implementation leader may, possibly, be a good project manager, but the right implementation leader will be competent in organizational behavior areas such as motivation for the adoption of new habits, minimizing the inevitable resistance to change, and accelerating the adoption of new practices while the business continues to operate.

The best candidate for implementation leader has the ability and experience to influence and lead the implementation plan as well as the desire and drive to accelerate the rollout and, in the end, leave a healthy, motivated organization. The ideal candidate has some of the following qualities:

- Understands change-management organizational behavior and adoption patterns.

- Is an effective motivating coach and can influence people they do not have authority over.

- Is a strong communicator, consensus builder, mediator, facilitator, teacher, and motivator, since the implementation leader will likely be interacting with the affected people throughout the organization more than anyone else. The implementation leader will likely have the largest opportunity to explain the "whys" and "hows" of the new strategy and to motivate the affected people to adopt the new plan.

- Can act as a role model and exhibit the behavior expected in the new business strategy.

- Can effectively coach senior executives in the organization on communication.

- Has credibility, trust, confidence, respect, and political connections with senior executives and the leaders of any mission-critical groups. These people may have to accept guidance from the implementation leader.

- Has a can-do problem-solving style to make tactical decisions quickly in order to accelerate the overall strategy implementation.

- Can make good decisions with less-than-complete information, which is often the case with a new strategy.

- Can escalate issues quickly to appropriate executives and push for resolution.

- Has sufficient understanding of the business to make tactical plans and decisions that will allow operations to continue during the rollout period.

- Understands project management, even though they may not be a project manager.

- Has the patience and understanding to interact with people who feel they are adversely affected and the aggressiveness to drive an accelerated implementation timetable without poisoning the work environment.

The implementation leader is usually someone from within the organization who has sufficient credibility and influence to effectively implement the business strategy. Nonetheless the role of implementation leader is usually new, with no established operating norms or past practices. This often gets overlooked because the experienced manager is a colleague the top executives have worked with before. It is important to articulate how the implementation leader will work with the senior team and the organization. Some topics to be expressed may include the following:

- Responsibilities: What are the responsibilities of the implementation leader?

- Expectations: What are the implementation's expected results and deadlines?

- Resources: What resources are available directly to the implementation leader (people and budget)?

- Tactical latitude and involvement: Which items in the business plan are sacred and which items does the implementation leader have some latitude to modify to accomplish the goal using the best possible method? How much involvement does the executive team want to have in the implementation?

- Reporting: What will be the format and timetable of progress updates?

- Escalation: What is the process to get quick resolution to any escalated issues?

Even though the new proposed business model may describe a highly optimized operation, getting from where you are today to the end point with the least amount of chaos requires a fair degree of change-management planning and execution expertise. A competent implementation leader will be able to help plan the implementation, identify the best implementation team, manage the rollout, create an environment that avoids generating organizational resistance, accelerate adoption, and leave an effective motivated organization when the new business strategy is implemented.

An example from the 1990s of a lack of implementation leadership comes to mind. At that time many large industrial firms were adopting the latest technology to improve maintenance practices and equipment reliability to ultimately improve production efficiency. The goal was to reduce production outages caused by equipment breakdown while simultaneously reducing maintenance costs. The technological solution that potentially allowed this efficiency improvement to take place was known as CMMS (computerized maintenance-management systems). By creating a state-of-the-art system and database of all maintained equipment, along with maintenance activities, predictive maintenance information, parts lists, breakdown records, meantime between failures, and repair costs, the firm could execute just-in-time maintenance, reduce production outages caused by equipment failure, and optimize the maintenance activities for maximum impact. Computerized maintenance-management systems were being deployed in many firms to replace traditional systems.

The strategy was good, and the business case demonstrated the benefits. The problem often was a lack of implementation leadership. Too many firms thought the main element of the strategy was the software and left the implementation to the "computer guy." In reality the key to implementation was a change in the overall maintenance strategy, a change in maintenance activities, and a new scheduling methodology. The software was simply the information-management tool. In many firms, a lack of an overall understanding of the change and the resulting lack of implementation leadership led to systems being launched but never fully utilized. Too often the CMMS software was loaded but the new approach didn't stick. The CMMS champion promised X percent ROI, but the old tried-and-true maintenance practices did not change. In some cases the implementation leader changed jobs (e.g., "the computer guy"); in other cases the maintenance work-order system was never changed to integrate into the new system. As a result, the new maintenance strategy utilizing CMMS did not generate the promised ROI. A diligent review of the implementation requirements, a review of the changes required, and an examination of the implementation leadership required would have identified the need for a strong implementation leader who understood organizational behavior. In hindsight, this complete analysis, which would have no doubt included a higher implementation cost, could have altered the original decision to adopt this new idea in the first place.

Document the Key Elements of the Implementation Plan Early

As you formulate your implementation or rollout plan, you will start to think about the tactical issues of executing your business strategy. Often the senior team will play a key part in the development of the implementation plans. Encourage their participation. Implementation planning sessions often surface issues that may be unclear or misunderstood in early general discussions of the strategy. Sometimes the creation of detailed end-point descriptions surface details of the strategy, of which various senior managers may have made differing interpretations or assumptions. The development of the implementation plans provides a forum for the senior team to ensure that they all have the same detailed interpretation. The implementation plan should clearly outline the step-by-step approach to implementing the new business strategy.

The documented implementation plan does not have to be a huge document or a formal document. This is a working document that can be presented *to* the senior team or *by* the senior team to employees. The detailed project management plans can be constructed later by the project manager and the implementation team and hopefully by members of the impacted groups in the organization.

The implementation plan should outline the key topics:

- How will the implementation be lead? Who will be the implementation leader? Will there be a project manager, a senior management steering team, or executive sponsors for particular portions of the plan? What will be their responsibilities and reporting relationships to one another? What will be the lines of communication?

- What milestones will be set, and what are the outcomes expected at each?

- What is the rollout strategy? Will it be implemented in phases? Will there be pilot projects? Will you run a parallel system for a period?

- What will be the major implementation stages if more than one?

- What target markets, divisions, business units, regions, or groups will be involved first, second, third, and so on? Is participation mandatory in these groups, or are you going to use sampling?

- If there will be pilot projects to fine-tune the strategy rollout, what groups will be involved, and how long will the pilots last?

- What will be the expectations of the first groups, and how will lessons learned be incorporated into the new business plan?

- What will be the problem-resolution escalation process?

Documenting the key elements of the implementation plan allows the senior team and mission-critical groups to "get on the same page" and clarify any misunderstanding before you launch your implementation activities. Sometimes, it is only when these items are written down that the true picture of the new strategy comes into focus for some people. Sometimes people only start to take ideas and plans seriously when they are documented. In any case, if we want to accelerate implementation activities, it is important to get hesitancy or confusion out of the way as early as possible to avoid pitfalls like the following:

- inaccurate information being communicated to the organization that will have to be corrected later, causing delays and creating the impression that the plan is changing on the go

- amplified delays involving a lot of people if we need to stop and sort things out once the organization is in transition

The implementation plan is not the communication plan. As we discuss later, the communication plan includes the need for change, the benefits of the new strategy, the key points of the new strategy, the details in the Compelling Attraction, the key elements of the implementation plan, and more.

Measure, Recognize, and Reward Implementation Progress

The points in the previous section outline what you plan to do, the order in which you plan to do it, who will be involved, and when you expect to reach certain milestones. The next step is to define a method to measure progress in the implementation. Most business strategies take some time to generate the expected business results, and in the meantime we want to measure progress en route to results. Progress-measurement metrics will be unique to each situation. You will likely have a variety of measurement parameters, many of which will be tactical in nature, such as the number of people trained or the number of systems that are fully functional in each pilot region.

The progress-measurement system will likely be fine-tuned as the implementation plan becomes more detailed. In large strategy implementations, it is necessary to have large project-management plans, which, if done well, can easily provide progress measurements and percentage completion for each implementation initiative or even progress tracking on a task-by-task basis. Most project-management software can easily provide progress and status reports.

Recognition and reward is a key part of accelerating the implementation of your business strategy. A good implementation plan and progress-measurement system provides you with the elements you need to recognize, reward, and motivate your employees. Conventional thinking is to reward results, not efforts. However, this is the place to reward efforts and contributions, because it is likely to be too early to see business results and we want to encourage people to embrace a new strategy that they may not be comfortable with yet.

Recognition and rewards do not necessarily involve a lot of money. Here are some tips to think about:

- As people start to adopt the new processes or exhibit the new desired behavior, recognize their progress.

- Recognize that some of the early adopters put at risk their career advancement, experienced peer alienation, and more. Reward them for their commitment and leadership.

- Recognize people who have made a large change in their role and lived through frustrations.

- Recognize early successes where progress is significant or results can be measured.

- Reward team leaders and people who provide big support.

- Recognition should be heralded at least among work-group employee peers or ideally throughout the appropriate parts of the whole organization.

- Recognition should be timely—as soon as possible after the progress is recognized.

- Recognition should specifically outline the progress the employee made.

Although cash awards are customary, rewards do not necessarily always involve bonus checks for large dollar amounts. A "thank you" letter from an executive and recognition in the company newsletter is a big start. When a group successfully adopts the new strategy, perhaps new uniforms, new colors, or new badges are appropriate recognition. Private recognition, such as a cash award, motivates the recipient. Public recognition can motivate a group. Recognition should be something that is visible to others of the growing number of people who are adopting the new strategy. Politicians use this during election campaigns—lawn signs are a method of displaying that other people are on your side—in an attempt to influence/ encourage you to get on their side.

A point of caution: A recognition-and-reward system can accelerate the strategy implementation. However, it will have little impact if the existing performance-measurement system is still in place and is contrary to the new business strategy. If a counterproductive reward system is in place, many managers, especially senior managers who typically have more at stake, will provide verbal support for the new strategy, but the implementation will not get out of the starting gate. This subversive resistance can generate major obstacles by influential people in the organization.

Get the Senior Team on One Common Message

An integral part of heightened implementation readiness is ensuring that all the senior managers are delivering the same message. The credibility of the new business strategy is improved if employees in the organization hear the same message being communicated over and over. The contrary is also true and unfortunately more common. If the organization's leadership team does not deliver a common strategy message or a common description of the intended outcomes, then the credibility of the message is severely wounded, confidence in the plan is weakened, and the communication effort will not inspire support in the organization. Generating support as quickly as possible is a key element of accelerating our implementation.

To help get the senior team on one common message I suggest two effective tools—the 100-Second Enlightenment message and the detailed description of the Compelling Attraction. We will talk more about these two tools later in the book. In some cases it may be a good idea to have a messaging session with the senior team to ensure that everyone understands the message and has a chance to ask for clarification about the details of the strategy, the consequences, and the end point. It is important to address questions here to get the core team on the same page. The core leadership team may have many questions themselves, which when answered and added to the message content will address questions employees will likely also have.

The Messaging Plan

The single most important success factor to accelerate the implementation of your business strategy is communication. This is the heart of aligning everyone's efforts on the new plan. They cannot support and align on a plan that they know little about or do not understand. Your communication plan can be your most influential strategy element to dispel employee uncertainty and accelerate adoption.

Here are the key objectives of the messaging plan:

- to inform the people in the organization

- to initiate acceptance of the new business strategy

- to set the stage for employees to support the new strategy

- to reduce the anxiety that comes from ambiguity and the turmoil of change

The messaging plan should not be left to the last minute. It requires some diligence to define a complete and effective communication plan. Often the details of the implementation plans are not yet worked out and many tactical issues of the business plan are yet to be defined. Nevertheless you must put the pieces of the story together as best as you can to build the content of your message plan. It will likely be necessary to include descriptions of what is "the most likely plan of action" or "the tentative plan of action." It is okay to point out elements of the plan that are not fully defined yet. It is not important to forecast every tactical detail, but if you leave out descriptions of major portions of the rollout, then employees will be left to draw their own conclusions or senior managers will provide explanations that are not necessarily consistent among the members of the leadership team. The message should answer the following employee questions as best as possible, given that many tactical issues are not fully defined yet:

- Why is it necessary to have a new business strategy? What is wrong with the status quo?

- What is the new business strategy and business plan?

- What other alternatives were considered, and why is this new strategy the best alternative?

- What are the benefits and expected outcomes of this new strategy that will make this change worthwhile?

- What will the end point look like? What will change in the business processes, organization, and responsibilities?

- What is the implementation or rollout plan?

- How will I be impacted personally—my job and my responsibilities, my work environment, my performance measurement, and my career?

- How will I be impacted during the implementation or transition period, and what are your expectations from me during this period?

- How do I find out more information, and whom do I ask questions?

There are many good publications on business communication, and we will not attempt to cover that topic comprehensively here. The list of questions above will give you a good start to define the content of your messaging plan, but the plan includes much more.

The checklist below can be a starting point to convert your message content into your messaging plan.

- complete stakeholder/constituency analysis—including expected objections and implementation challenges

- announcement plan

- key messages, as outlined in the list above

- 100-Second Enlightenment (more on this in later in the book)

- medium and presentation mix (remember that not everyone effectively receives information the same way—some need to hear it explained, some understand best with analogies, some need diagrams to help understand, some need to take information away and quietly reread it, and so on)

- face-time plan (remember that top-management consistency gives the message authority and commitment, but a message from frontline management and direct supervisors gives the message credibility)

- timetable

- methods of gathering feedback and evaluating communication success

One final point on your messaging plan: Our individual limits are all different, but people can only absorb information so fast and in finite quantities. There may also be some implementation details and actions that your employees will absorb only after they understand and accept the new strategy initiatives. This may seem in conflict with the point above about giving the best descriptions possible, but it is not. Give your employees as much detail as possible to build the credibility of the plan, but not to the point of overwhelming them with information. With this in mind, your messaging plan may have several phases. Later phases will inform your employees about the details of the new business strategy and plan so they can start to align their activities in support of the new strategy and make tactical decisions that are aligned with the implementation plans.

Your message plan is your medium, your tool, to convert the new strategy from ideas and analysis into advocacy and action in the organization. This will be a major and critical element to accelerate the implementation of your new business strategy. If you only do one thing right, this is it.

A Few Points, from Experience, about Implementation Readiness

Don't Underestimate the Amount of Management Time Required

There is a lot of management time, at all levels, required to implement a major business initiative or change. If the new business strategy is going to become part of the "normal" way things are done and engrained in the activities, systems, and culture, then the management team has two responsibilities: first, to lead the change in their area or department; and second, to change some of their own practices as well.

It should be clear to all levels of management that the executive team expects all managers to make the time to embrace the necessary changes, expects all managers to participate in leading the implementation efforts, and expects all managers to recognize the time required to implement the new business strategy.

The challenge is not always in the middle and frontline management. The executive team sometimes visualizes a new initiative or organization change but is unaware of the complexity or the amount of work required in altering systems, redefining processes, rewriting procedures, training people, and communicating the change. Ensure that you have adequate resources in place to manage the implementation and change process.

Recognize That Change Management Is Not an Exact Science

Implementing a new business strategy is all about change management. Change management combines the art of leadership, the psychology of organizational behavior, the skills of project management, and much more. Change management often takes a functional organization with orchestrated processes and launches that organization into a period of unsynchronized turmoil. Change management is as abstract as leadership and requires similar level of skills and experience. Change management is not a simple matter of putting a puzzle back together again and ending up with a reinvented high-performing business. Change management is not an exact science. Accelerating implementation plans pushes the boundaries of change management.

Here are a few thoughts on accelerated business strategies and change management:

- Even with the best talent leading your accelerated business-strategy implementation, mistakes will be made.

- Balance being intuitive with being analytical.

- Accept that the nature of change has some degree of disorderliness.

- Give credit to those who took the risk and participated early—hold them harmless from any downside.

- Leadership must take ownership/accountability for problems and not go on a witch hunt. To foster a supportive culture of the change, the change agents must feel as though they are protected and free to take the necessary risks and to go out on a limb.

- When necessary, back up and fix problems or mistakes and then move on.

- Accept and prepare for the fact that change introduces uncertainty.

Don't Shortcut—Give Them Time to Accept New Ideas

As senior management prepare to announce their new business strategy, there is often a feeling of eagerness to launch into action; after all you have been analyzing and planning this for some time, and it feels like it is time to do something. We need to make sure that we don't lose sight of the fact that the majority of the people in the organization have not had a chance to understand and accept the new strategy, and therefore it is unlikely that they are ready to enthusiastically support it.

People need time, a grace period, to accept new ideas. The amount of time will vary depending on how much impact the new idea has on them or how dramatic the change is. Acceptance of new ideas is rarely instantaneous. Acceptance means letting go of the old and familiar, which may not happen easily, and accepting the new. People need time to understand the change, maybe get over the news if it was a shock, ask questions, clarify, and think about how they will be affected. They need an acceptance period—even a brief one. Don't be fooled by the lack of objections in the beginning. There is a huge difference between not objecting to a new idea and embracing an idea to the point where it alters someone's behavior. To accelerate the implementation of your new strategy, you will not only need acceptance of the ideas in the new approach but also active support to aggressively implement the changes required for the new business approach.

If the people don't accept the need for change and accept the new business strategy, then your implementation efforts will be much more difficult and you can look forward to facing halfhearted implementation efforts and a lot of repeated questions like "What is the purpose or benefit in doing this?" Without fundamental acceptance of the need for change, your implementations efforts are likely to be burdened with frustration and disappointing results. You may even see high-potential people leave the organization.

An example comes to mind. This is a simple change, but it exemplifies the point. A service company was planning to move their office from one area of Montreal to a location at the other end of the city. This would mean a much longer commute to the office for some employees, but it would position the office closer to the majority of the company's core customers. This was explained to all the employees. Initially a number of employees were not happy with the longer commute they would face at the beginning and end of each day, although they recognized the rationale for the move. The management team took several weeks (an acceptance period) to answer questions from employees and get their feedback on issues that should be considered in the new site location. Many employees could have easily left for competitive jobs in the same industry, but not one person left. Morale remained high, and in the end, the service company was able to improve customer service and be more successful from the new location. The grace period allowed the service employees to accept the new ideas.

Involve Target Groups in the Planning

Involve people in the target groups as much as possible. It not only helps extinguish "not invented here" but also creates a sense of self-worth and ownership and ultimately will likely lead to better informed decisions—especially on the implementation plan. One of the biggest resistance factors is that the plan doesn't fit me or my group, that someone is trying to whitewash a standard solution in areas where it does not fit rather than design the solution to optimize the way each group accomplishes the desired outcomes.

Let's think back to the computerized maintenance-management system (CMMS) we explored earlier. The skilled trade people and the management of the maintenance team were key to the success of the new maintenance strategy. Their early involvement could have identified obstacles and certainly could have enlisted their support and expertise to make the new approach successful.

Part II

An Accelerator's Tool Kit

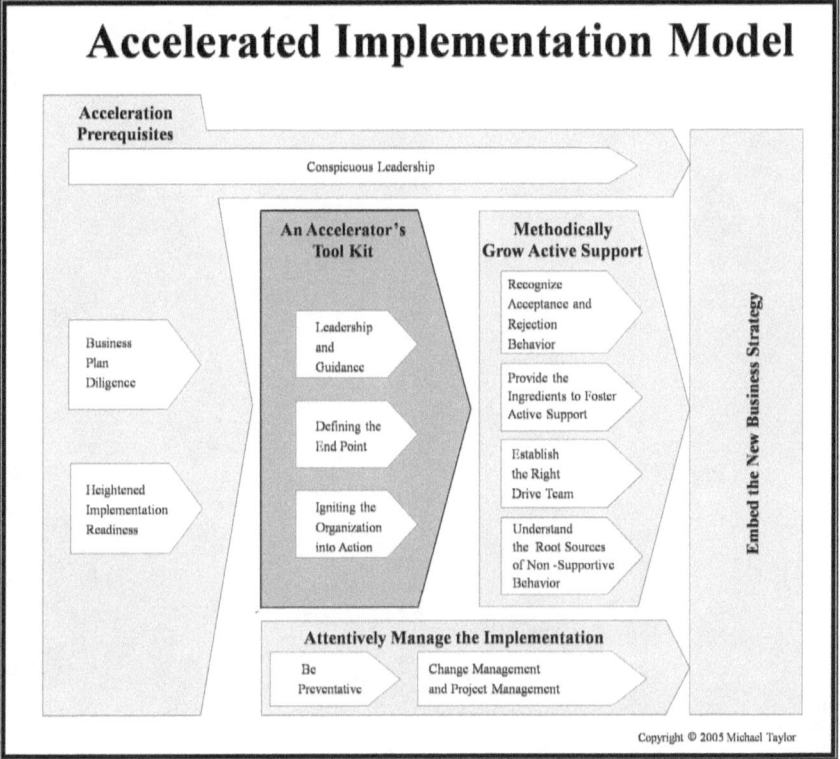

Accelerated Implementation Model

Acceleration Prerequisites

Conspicuous Leadership

An Accelerator's Tool Kit

Methodically Grow Active Support

Business Plan Diligence

Leadership and Guidance

Recognize Acceptance and Rejection Behavior

Provide the Ingredients to Foster Active Support

Defining the End Point

Establish the Right Drive Team

Heightened Implementation Readiness

Igniting the Organization into Action

Understand the Root Sources of Non-Supportive Behavior

Embed the New Business Strategy

Attentively Manage the Implementation

Be Preventative

Change Management and Project Management

Copyright © 2005 Michael Taylor

Introduction

An accelerated business-strategy implementation requires the organization to quickly accept new ideas and aggressively engage in the implementation. This does not happen automatically. As we will discuss in later chapters, the process of growing from acceptance to engaged support takes time and effort. However, there are some tools we can prepare that will help people in the organization with the adoption process—ultimately accelerating adoption and implementation.

In this section we will discuss the role of leadership and describe several of the accelerator's tools, such as the "Compelling Attraction" and the "100-Second Enlightenment." In this section, we will discuss these three elements:

- *Leadership and Guidance*: Leading a business change amplifies the need for organizational leadership. We will describe the need for guidance to explain the new business strategy, the expected outcome, and why the new plan is better than the existing approach, and to unite the organization to implement the new strategy.

- *Defining the End Point*: A Compelling Attraction to clarify and synchronize what everyone is working toward and to motivate the organization; and a 100-Second Enlightenment: a synopsis that pulls the message all together

- *Igniting the Organization to Action:* An Igniting Event to spark the organization into action and synchronize their efforts onto one action plan

Chapter 4

Leadership and Guidance

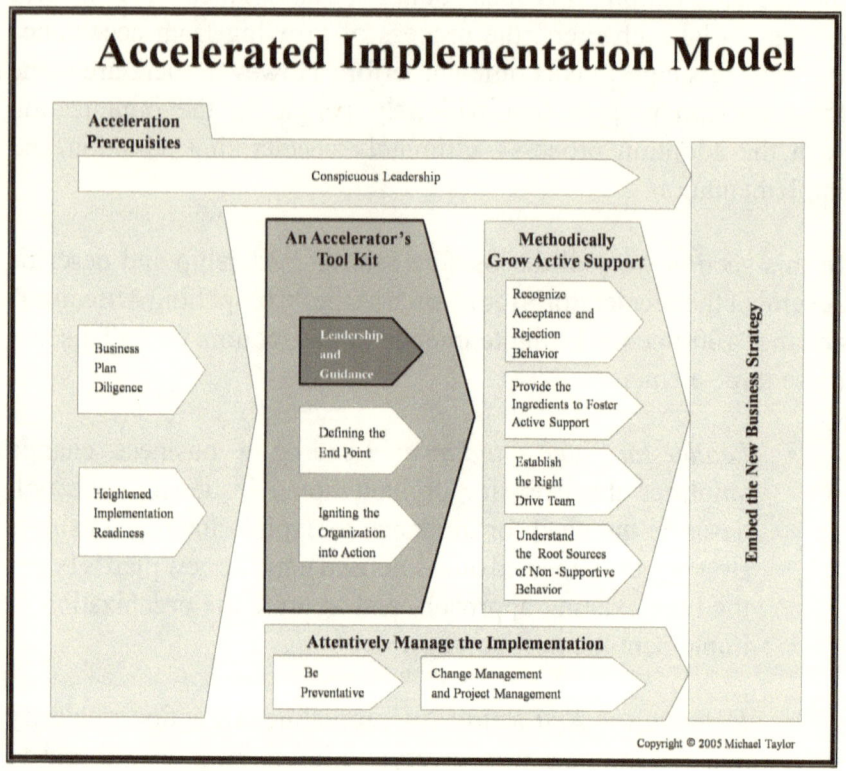

Accelerated Implementation Model

Acceleration Prerequisites

Conspicuous Leadership

An Accelerator's Tool Kit

Methodically Grow Active Support

Business Plan Diligence

Leadership and Guidance

Recognize Acceptance and Rejection Behavior

Provide the Ingredients to Foster Active Support

Defining the End Point

Establish the Right Drive Team

Heightened Implementation Readiness

Igniting the Organization into Action

Understand the Root Sources of Non-Supportive Behavior

Embed the New Business Strategy

Attentively Manage the Implementation

Be Preventative

Change Management and Project Management

Copyright © 2005 Michael Taylor

Guidance, Confidence, and Credibility

The announcement of the new business strategy is the first opportunity for many people in the organization to rally in support of the new plan, or alternatively, the announcement can initiate anxiety, defensiveness, and opposition to the new direction in which the organization is going.

People in the organization rely on the company's leaders to set the direction of the organization as well as organize and manage the resources of the company to execute business strategies. Your announcement of the new business strategy will be an invitation for the people in the organization to follow the new direction you have set. Change always sparks some anxiety. The announcement of a new business strategy is an opportunity to develop confidence and early support in the new business strategy as well as confidence in your leadership capability to make the new plan successful.

There is certain content that should be in an initial strategy announcement to reduce anxiety and bolster confidence in the new strategic ideas: an explanation of why the status quo is unacceptable, a description of the analysis that led to the new business strategy, a relatively detailed picture of the destination, a summary of the changes required, and a summary of the expected beneficial outcomes. In addition to explaining the business rationale, the announcement should indicate how people will be affected and how they will fit into the new business approach. Once the content and the impact of the new strategy is explained, the most important factor, and the one most commonly overlooked, is a description of how you will implement the changes. This is your opportunity to develop the confidence that the plan is achievable, which is a strong ingredient to boost early acceptance of the new strategy and ideas.

At this stage in the accelerated strategy implementation, the challenge is not "getting things started or done." The challenge is to provide the people in the organization with the knowledge of what is going to happen and to develop confidence in the leadership's ability to execute the new approach successfully. If the organization does not have the confidence in the leader's ability to successfully implement the new strategy, they are unlikely to support the leadership or the new business plan. A successful kickoff announcement can go a long way toward inspiring confidence in the leader's ability to successfully implement the new strategy. As mentioned earlier, the organization will look for credibility in the business strategy and the implementation plan as indicators of credibility in the leader.

In the weeks and months that follow, the organization will watch the behavior and actions of the leader and the management team to see if their behavior supports the new business plan or if their behavior ignores the new business plan in favor of the status quo. The organization will look for any sign that the business strategy was simply a "program of the month" and not a real sustained strategy. They will look for any sign that the plan is drifting from the original strategy or vision. They will look for the leader's tolerance of those who deliberately opt out of the new strategy, contravene the new strategy, or manipulate the new strategy for their personal benefit. Provided that the business plan review confirmed the validity of the strategy and the leader is not deaf to legitimate feedback, a strong commitment to the strategy will strengthen the confidence in the leader's ability to be successful with the new strategy.

A note of caution: The acceptance of new ideas, especially ideas requiring dramatic or widespread change, can be difficult for many people. The information in the announcement can be overwhelming. It can be a lot of information for the people in your organization to digest. You want them to absorb and understand it. We will discuss the acceptance and adoption process later, but it is important to note here that no one can drink out of a fire hose. You need to provide this information at a pace that allows for acceptance of new ideas before building on that foundation.

If the people in your organization understand your business plan, believe in the merits of the business plan, and have confidence in the leadership and the organization to implement it, then you have created a strong foundation for an accelerated implementation.

Empower a Culture of Change

Igniting the organization to accelerate the new strategy implementation requires an empowered organization ready to participate and contribute to driving the implementation of the new strategy. This requires a motivated and empowered organization. Faith in the leadership and the new strategy are prerequisites, but the participants need to be free to change from the old methods without risk. They need to know that they won't suffer poor performance appraisals or lose incentive compensation by adopting the new plan.

They need to be free to join task forces and ad hoc teams without risk of missing a career opportunities or falling out of favor with their direct manager.

Accelerating a new business strategy requires pushing the envelope a little. You don't want to promote carefree experimentation, but it is must be safe to take some risks rather than wait for every move to be proven, guaranteed safe, or waiting for the approval of many levels of management. The frontline managers need to be able to act unilaterally on tactical issues to accelerate adoption. They need to alter project plans, rethink purchasing decisions, and adjust employee objectives.

To accelerate your strategy implementation, the whole organization needs to start adopting as quickly as possible, which means that everyone must contribute to driving the change. If you have done a good job of communicating a detailed picture of what you are building, a good job of communicating the implementation plan, and a good job of identifying the key success factors, then the people in the organization will be able to make tactical decisions that are more or less aligned with the new plan. It will not be perfect—many people working in parallel, assuming sensible risk, will make some mistakes. This is the cost of acceleration. If the people in the organization can embrace this culture of change, then the adoption rate will be accelerated.

Active and Participatory Sponsorship

Active and participatory sponsorship, by the leadership team, fuels acceleration. The best way to guide and motivate is to be conspicuously out in front of the people you are leading. Be active sponsors of the new business strategy and demonstrate your support by being visibly involved, inspect the progress, answer questions, and coach performance. Remember that the organization views a broad span of management to be the "leadership." The 100-Second Enlightenment, described later in this section, should be actively promoted and virtually identical from every senior manager. Every senior manager's support should be conspicuously out front and visible to set the stage for an accelerated adoption of the new business plan.

A Tip, from Experience

There Is No Substitute for a Live-in-Person Address from the Leader

The organization's leadership must communicate directly to the groups they want to motivate—particularly the CEO or business leader. This may seem obvious, but far too often this is done by correspondence or e-mail or referral to a Web site. This is a time to communicate face-to-face, to provide guidance, to demonstrate commitment, to relieve anxiety, to empower change managers, to generate enthusiasm, and to spark people into action. There is no substitute for a live-in-person address from the leader. The people in the organization can witness the passion, commitment, and confidence in your voice and your body language. You can bolster confidence by being open to questions and discussion. Open discussion also helps people feel a connection to the new plan.

Sometimes a letter or e-mail is the only way to communicate to widely distributed organizations. However, we need to recognize that a letter or e-mail is a one-way communication and can easily be perceived as a plan being forced on the people in the organization.

Communicate live—directly to the people—whenever and as often as possible. Perhaps a full population meeting can be conducted. Smaller meetings are more effective; town hall–style interactive meetings are very especially effective, especially in decentralized organizations where senior executive visits are not frequent.

Chapter 5

Defining the End Point

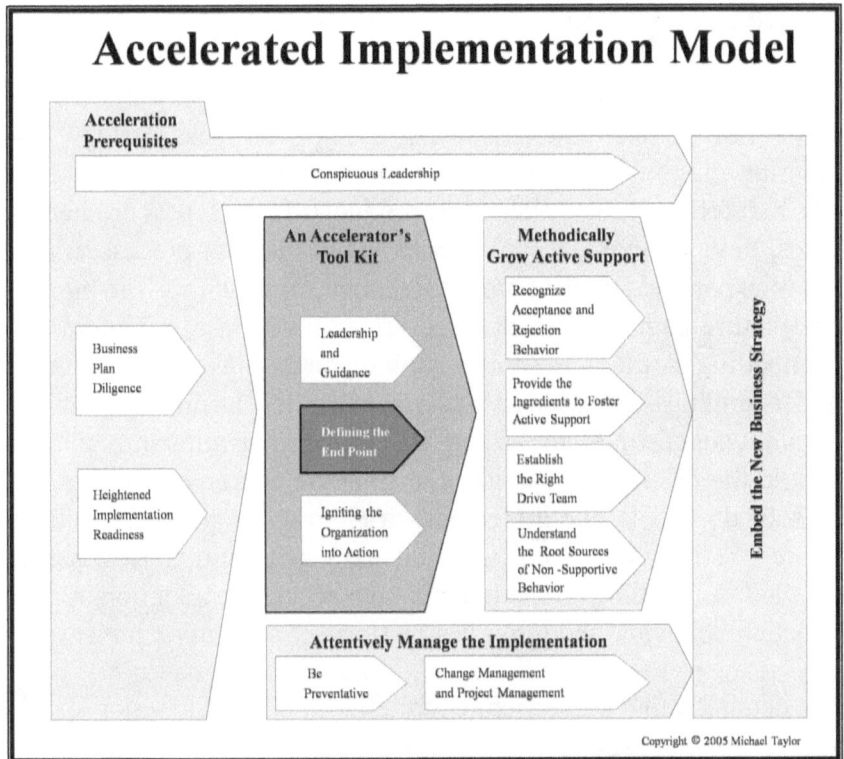

The Compelling Attraction

Sir Isaac Newton postulated, "A body moving in one direction will continue in that direction unless a force is applied to change that direction." Let's make one small change to Newton's famous law of physics. Let's exchange the word "body" for the word "organization," and we have what we might call a law of organizational behavior. "An organization moving in one direction will continue in that direction unless a force is applied to change that direction."

To effectively change the direction of a business organization, we must influence the people in the organization to change their direction; that is, their behavior, processes, priorities, and work habits. The most effective way to accomplish this is to motivate them to make the change. The most effective way to motivate the organization to change is to give them a new Compelling Attraction to work toward.

The Compelling Attraction is a detailed explanation, a mind's-eye picture, of the desired end result of the new business strategy. The description should be as detailed as possible, including such things as new marketing or sales plans, new product offerings, new production plans, new technology applications, new business processes, new job roles, or the details of a new organization structure. The mind's-eye picture should be as detailed as possible. At a minimum, the Compelling Attraction should provide everyone with a detailed understanding of the desired outcome of the new business initiatives. I am not suggesting that the people in the organization only need to be told the destination and all your implementation challenges will be solved. This is one ingredient—a potentially potent ingredient. There is still a lot of change management required. However, a detailed Compelling Attraction will help accelerate adoption, reduce rejection behavior, and provide a platform for smoother transitions.

The detailed mind's-eye picture of the Compelling Attraction should address several aspects:

- The Compelling Attraction should clearly outline the benefits of the new strategy, for the business as well as for the people involved. This explanation should be sufficiently detailed so the affected people in the organization can identify how their department or they personally will be impacted and will benefit. Not all quantifiable details will be known in early planning stages, but the benefits should be described as best as possible.

- A detailed picture of the Compelling Attraction will reduce the unknown, reduce the associated anxiety, and take the first steps toward avoiding organizational resistance to the new business plan. One of the largest factors that create resistance to change is the anxiety created from not knowing what lies ahead. This is perhaps the most important element of the Compelling Attraction. Large parts of the population will gravitate toward the known, even at a cost of overtly ignoring new instructions, rather than step into uncertain futures and unknown outcomes. People often find comfort in the predictability of their daily routines. To get them to become more comfortable with a new business structure or model, it is important to reduce their anxiety by painting a detailed picture in their mind's eye of the expected outcome. This mind's-eye picture allows the impacted people in the organization to see their role, their fit, and their personal situation in the new business strategy.

- Some people are ill at ease with change and will always prefer the comfort of the status quo. The Compelling Attraction needs to outline the unattractive projected future if the organization remains on the existing path. Your description will point out the problems with the status quo and help encourage this portion of the population to be open to considering new alternatives.

- A Compelling Attraction can not only help avoid organizational resistance but can also initiate early support and motivation for the new business strategy. In almost all cases, there are some people in the organization who are always looking for better solutions. For these people, the Compelling Attraction should demonstrate why the chosen business strategy best fits the market, the competitive environment, and the organizational situation. The Compelling Attraction can encourage these people to become advocates and active supporters.

- A detailed picture will provide one common understanding and interpretation of the desired end point. The mind's-eye picture of the Compelling Attraction requires considerable detail. If you introduce new ideas without sufficient details, you will allow everyone to interpret the new ideas and visualize the details with their own perspective. Every person will have their own different interpretation, focused on themselves, often assuming the worst impact for themselves. These individual interpretations can germinate the seeds of reluctance rather than support. Although a lot of people will likely try to understand how the new strategy will impact the business, human nature will result in everyone interpreting how they will be impacted personally. If you don't provide a detailed picture, they will create one in their own mind. One common understanding and interpretation will provide a foundation for aligned implementation activities later. A detailed picture will not create instant support, but it will help avoid later delays due to confusion or misunderstanding.

The detailed Compelling Attraction will undoubtedly start with why change is necessary as well as the overall goals and strategy, but it must end with details of expected tactical impacts such as expected changes to job roles and responsibilities, changes to key processes, changes to organizational structures, and changes to work environments or locations.

The early support of influential frontline employees often proves key to accelerating early adoption and implementation. The explanation should be detailed enough to be credible with these important frontline people. Experienced people in the organization will look for critical evidence:

- commitment of resources

- the capability to make the changes you have outlined in the detailed picture

- early evidence of real change taking place—not just lip service

It is helpful to highlight critical information to establish the credibility of the new initiatives. The detailed explanation should refer to your market research and link it to the need for change. The strongest credibility for the new business strategy will be generated if the people in the organization can clearly see how their tactical efforts contribute to the overall business strategy, such as profitability, market-share growth, or customer satisfaction.

The Compelling Attraction needs to be as specific and detailed as possible. You may not have all the details yet, but predict as best as you can. If you are having real difficulty creating a detailed description of the end point you are striving for, then perhaps your business plan diligence is not complete. In management we sometimes become accustomed to dealing with abstract ideas. We sometimes view our organizations as a complex web of processes and stockpiles. Not everyone views the world that way. Be as specific as possible with your detailed mind's-eye picture. Help your people understand the end point with a detailed description of what the organization and their work life will be like after the completion of the new initiatives. Your people will start to view how they will personally be impacted and likely start to ask questions of clarification. Your guidance to help understand the new business model in a meticulous way helps build credibility, helps clarify the fine points of the implementation plan, and sets the stage for people in the organization to contribute to the rollout in their area.

Make your descriptions motivating. Take the opportunity to point out the benefits of the new course of action. Use the detailed mind's-eye description to create a Compelling Attraction. This may be the time you want to empathize with the challenges that lie ahead and the difficulty of adopting new ways and means. If you can successfully guide people to understand what you are trying to build and motivate them to want to build it, you have taken a large step forward in preparing for an accelerated implementation.

An added benefit of creating a detailed picture of the future outcome is the opportunity to really understand the resource requirements. If you have a solid understanding of the expected tactical end point of the rollout, then you can understand the number of people required, the skills required, the equipment required, and the facilities required. Hopefully you can easily take that planning to the next level and foresee the support and infrastructure required, such as training, performance measurement systems, IT systems, security, and a whole host of other systems.

The 100-Second Enlightenment

The detailed explanation of the organization's goals and business plan outlined in the Compelling Attraction is a key element of preparedness. It addresses many aspects of the end point of the new business strategy. It serves to make sure everyone is working toward the same model and to alleviate some of the anxiety of an unknown future. However, until people in the organization are interested in the new business strategy, they are unlikely to pay a lot of attention to long addresses or read long communications. It is important to grab the organization's attention and start them thinking about the new business strategy. You need a brief and impactful message to explain your goal and outline your plan. This is the 100-Second Enlightenment.

We are all familiar with the evening news sound bite. Some of our most prominent political leaders become masters at taking complex plans and distilling those plans into a sound bite that encapsulates the objective of their plan, why it is important, and how it will be executed. They work hard on the sound-bite approach because it works. In business we are not vying for a five-second sound bite on the evening news, but we are vying for the attention of our people, who have a lot on their mind. I have coached people to think about encapsulating your business goal into one sentence followed with a 100-second explanation.

Encapsulating your business goal into a one-sentence sound bite can prove to be a challenge. It must be specific and not simply a motherhood statement. Stating that you want to "grow sales and improve profits" is motherhood. It is better to be as specific as possible. For example: "We want to increase market share to become number two in the western region and keep margins above 15 percent." Avoid stretching the goal into a detailed story of your objectives for product lines, sales districts, and so on.

Your intention is to establish simplicity of purpose that the organization can identify with and unite behind. The goal should be specific enough so people in the organization can identify how their activities contribute to the goals. The goals should not be open-ended, such as "improve profits." They should have a benchmark that people can identify with, such as "profit margins above 15 percent."

A colleague once told me he had a rule he used when balancing motherhood generalities and becoming too detailed. My colleague used to tell me it had to be suitable for spouses and board members. He claimed employees shared news from work with their spouses, and that spouses had only a passing interest in the details the employee brought home from the office. If it was too detailed, the spouse was not interested. On the other hand, the goal cannot be motherhood. My colleague argued that board members want to be confident that your goals are not simply motherhood statements but rather that they are specific enough to lead to a business strategy. I have used this convenient acid test many times to help encapsulate business goals into a single sentence—suitable for spouses and board members.

Why a one-sentence goal and why 100 seconds? If the goal or outcome cannot be explained in one sentence, it is likely not concise enough to be accepted by a large group. This goal should become the mantra that frontline managers and supervisors are routinely repeating to their people. The goal should become a mantra that everyone can unite behind.

The 100-Second Enlightenment statement is more than your one-sentence goal. It is also an encapsulated explanation of the business strategy designed to generate interest so that your employees want to learn more.

The explanation of the goal should take no more than 100 seconds; otherwise it is too complex for some of the same reasons mentioned above. People need to absorb it quickly. Why 100 seconds? Because that is a reasonable attention span for someone who may not be interested in listening to more details yet. We want to use the 100-Second Enlightenment to generate some curiosity to listen to the more detailed Compelling Attraction. It will be necessary at some point to go into more depth with a detailed explanation, but first you must get their interest. Once you have their attention, the details in the Compelling Attraction will give the 100-Second Enlightenment credibility.

When you are communicating the goals and 100-Second Enlightenment, if possible, allow time for questions. Questions will allow more in-depth descriptions of plans, background, and research to be explained.

A limit of 100 seconds does not seem like a lot of time to communicate why the status quo is not acceptable, what market forces are impacting your business, what your goals and your strategy are, and to hint at the end point and the benefits of your new plan. This seems like a lot to cover in 100 seconds, but it is amazing how much you can communicate in such a short time. The 100-Second Enlightenment should be a written document in the communication plan. Start with the key points in each of the areas mentioned above, prioritize the key points in each section, and then test it for length. Make sure you say it out loud. It takes longer to say it out loud than in your head. Saying it out loud also forces you to thread your key points into sentences and ultimately into a story, a message.

Your 100-second story will be brief enough to allow your people to remember the key points. Often you will want your managers to repeat and disseminate the plan to the people in their organization. A long, complex rationalization is sure to lose the impact of the message and likely to get mixed up in the process. A 100-second description is more likely to stay intact and have impact. This will improve the consistency of the message, which helps build credibility.

A strong message in your 100-Second Enlightenment can spark interest, understanding, and curiosity about the new business plan. This will lead to questions, clarification, and discussion, which, now that you have their attention, will allow more opportunity to explain the detailed picture of the Compelling Attraction. The 100-Second Enlightenment is the spark to kick off the communication process— that is why I call it the 100-Second Enlightenment.

A clear 100-Second Enlightenment statement and the details of the Compelling Attraction give everyone in the organization a common purpose and understanding. This provides the foundation for less-chaotic organizational change. It allows the organization to transform rather than have people simply start doing different and now unconnected new tasks. As individuals change their work structure, role, and activities, they must interact with others in new not-yet-created process links. The common purpose of the overall goal and the common understanding of the Compelling Attraction will allow then to make good decisions that fit the overall new business model.

An Example, from Experience, about Defining the End Point

Make the Compelling Attraction Sufficiently Detailed to Be Useful

It sounds foolish to say "just tell them your vision and they will adapt in harmony." However, this is sometimes what happens. Very early in my career I was a marketing analyst in a large multinational. The division I was in was being beaten badly by competition. A new strategy was launched by the divisional executive team. We were going to reposition and move upscale in the market. We were going to provide the market with a higher-value offering in hopes of being able to sell on value rather than low price. We were not the low-cost supplier, and we needed to differentiate ourselves in the market. Moving to a higher-value position in the market was the only option at the time. Unfortunately, the strategy ended there. Moving to a higher-value position is a goal, not a strategy. No strategy was presented. There was no detailed picture of the destination we were striving for; there was no coaching on how to get there, no unified plan. Everyone in the organization had their own interpretation of what to do, and in the end the lack of a unified effort resulted in no change from the status quo. The strategy was not sufficiently detailed to be implementable. In hindsight, I think the development of a detailed picture of the end point would have forced more detailed planning to take place.

Chapter 6

Igniting the Organization into Action

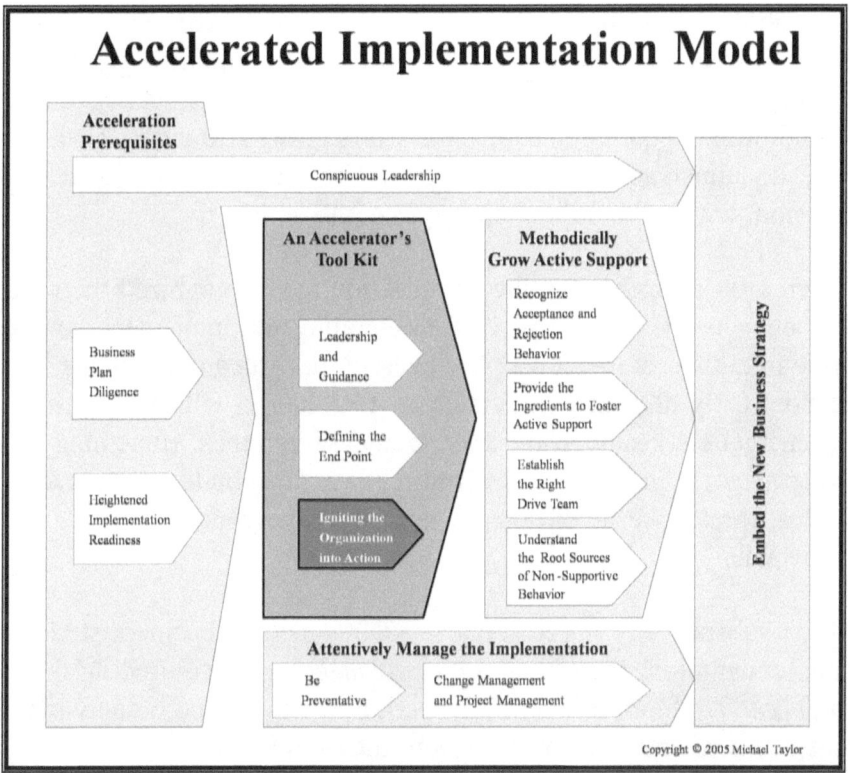

An Igniting Event

When should we announce our new plans? When should we launch? These are typical questions and good questions. The executive team often wants to get under way as fast as possible, and rightly so—time is money. The implementation team often prefers to wait, often until more preparations are done or until more resources are in place. There will always be a reason why you should delay the launch to a later time, but there will never be an ideal time. At some point you need to pull the trigger and launch. The important point is to be ready. When you pull the trigger and make the launch announcements, be ready to use the energy and enthusiasm that is created by the launch to accelerate early adoption. It is sometimes best to have a launch announcement followed, after a short break, by a kickoff session. The initial launch announcement is not a simple thing. It should have all the details of the Compelling Attraction. The short time in between announcement and kickoff allows some time of acceptance. This short time can vary from a few minutes to several days, depending on the complexity of the changes required. In addition to communicating the Compelling Attraction, you can use the launch announcement to plan who should attend the kickoff session, which should ignite everyone into action.

Even after the people in the organization have recognized the need for change, the hardest part of accelerating the implementation of new initiatives is to get people sincerely motivated and moving into action. Only after they fully support the change will they be ready to energetically support the new strategy. Even then, something has to spark them into action. An Igniting Event can build energy, create focus, create a sense of urgency, and reset everyone's efforts to one timetable.

To substantially accelerate your new business-strategy implementation, more than a kickoff *meeting* is required. Make it an *event*. An Igniting Event can spark new energy and broadly plant the seeds of enthusiasm throughout the organization. Your Igniting Event should accomplish the following goals:

- Repeat or summarize

  o why the status quo is unacceptable using the convincing data available.

  o the 100-Second Enlightenment (repetition is a good way for this to become the organization's mantra).

  o the Compelling Attraction.

- Instill a sense of urgency.

- Spark the people involved into synchronized action.

Many organizations suffer from program fatigue. If the organization has seen a stream of changes from a series of executives, after a while a new business strategy seems more like another "program of the month" and consequently gets little attention. If this is evident in your organization, the biggest enemy is not lethargy; the biggest enemies are complacency and indifference. The easiest and most comfortable reaction for employees is often to do nothing and to change nothing in the hopes that this new initiative will pass like the ones before it. If done well, an Igniting Event can jolt the organization out of complacency and spark concern and interest.

A general employee meeting with senior management announce-ments about new corporate goals is not an Igniting Event. News of a further trend in downward results may prove not to ignite enthusiasm, because it can be questioned why this was not a problem when someone saw this trend developing before. Sometimes the best Igniting Event is a combination of things. A new technology, a new revelation of analysis, or new market information can refresh the need to make a change now. This can then generate a sense of urgency if combined with the goal of implementing the resulting new strategy by a fixed date with defined results. The combination of something new and an urgency to react is a convincing and igniting spark to create enthusiasm and spur people into action. Keep in mind that enthusiasm evaporates, so don't set the substantial completion date too far in the future. A sense of urgency has limits.

A management or an employee meeting is often the setting for an Igniting Event. Use the opportunity to introduce many influencers and thought leaders in the organization to the 100-Second Enlightenment and the seeds of enthusiasm. An Igniting Event alone is a wasted opportunity. Without a diligent business plan, leadership readiness, a Compelling Attraction, and an encapsulated 100-Second Enlightenment explanation, the energy generated from an Igniting Event will likely dissipate quickly.

Be prepared and drive into actions immediately. It is counterproductive to go to the effort of creating a sense of urgency and not be ready to discuss actions, assign responsibilities, set objectives and milestones, and lay out the implementation strategy.

Ignition Preparation and Timing

Consider the timing of the Igniting Event. Are you ready to launch into action? Do you have a critical mass of executive support? Are the prerequisites mentioned in the previous sections in place? A false start will make it much harder to generate enthusiasm for any later restarts.

The announcement that "we can no longer continue as we are and we need to change" causes immediate anxiety in the organization. It is the senior management's responsibility to provide guidance, direction, motivation, and a structured plan to be successful. Any change will cause people to be apprehensive, uncertain, and anxious. They will look for leadership to help provide confidence and direction. The executive management must communicate directly with the people to provide that leadership. They must communicate the merits of the plan and demonstrate their commitment to work through the adversity of change. The executive management is not just the CEO. The whole executive team must be supportive, since they are perceived as being "on the inside loop of information." This can be a turning point for an organization, when either enthusiasm or resistance is created. Preparation makes the difference. Communicate the sense of urgency to drive quickly into actions and have a structured implementation strategy to spark people into a synchronized rollout. It is healthy to use the kickoff session to define the details of the early implementation steps. This can create a sense of ownership and commitment. It can also result in better plans that can be implemented faster.

Part III

Methodically Grow Active Support

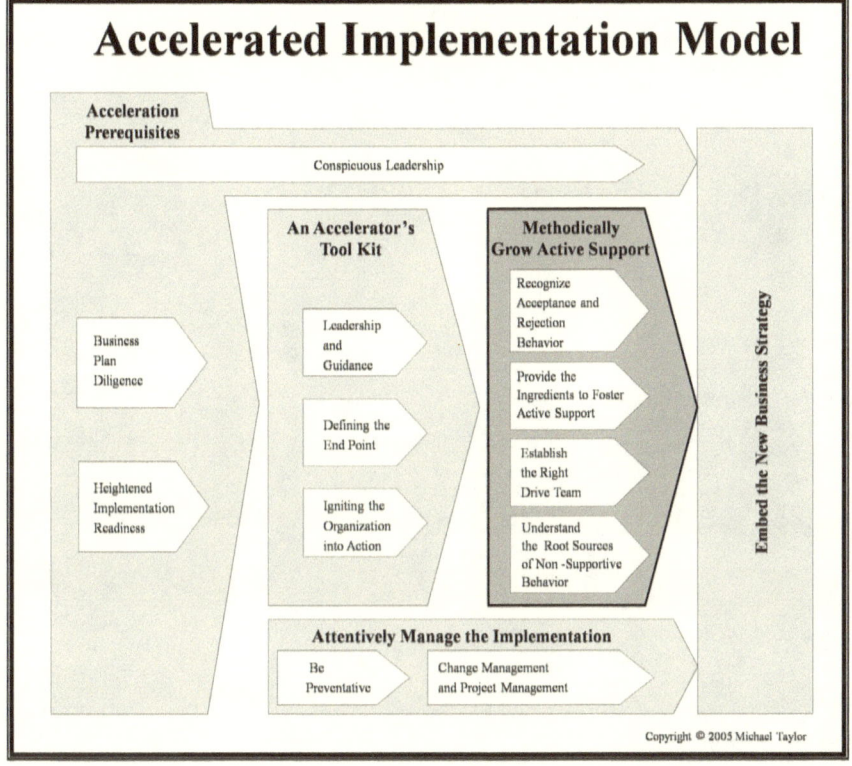

Accelerated Implementation Model

Acceleration Prerequisites

Conspicuous Leadership

An Accelerator's Tool Kit

Methodically Grow Active Support

Business Plan Diligence

Leadership and Guidance

Recognize Acceptance and Rejection Behavior

Provide the Ingredients to Foster Active Support

Defining the End Point

Establish the Right Drive Team

Heightened Implementation Readiness

Igniting the Organization into Action

Understand the Root Sources of Non-Supportive Behavior

Embed the New Business Strategy

Attentively Manage the Implementation

Be Preventative

Change Management and Project Management

Copyright © 2005 Michael Taylor

Introduction

Growing strong support is the foundation of implementing any new idea. As the title of this section implies, support is not instantaneous—you must grow support. However, we want more than passive support. To accelerate the implementation of a new strategy, we need *active* support. In this section we will discuss the process of methodically growing active support to accelerate business-strategy implementation. The process starts with accepting the fact that the status quo is unacceptable and ends with varying degrees of support—or opposition.

In the following chapters we explore the elements to methodically grow active support:

- Recognize acceptance and rejection behavior.

- Provide the ingredients to foster active support.

- Establish the right drive team.

- Understand the root sources of non-supportive behavior.

Chapter 7

Recognize Acceptance and Rejection Behavior

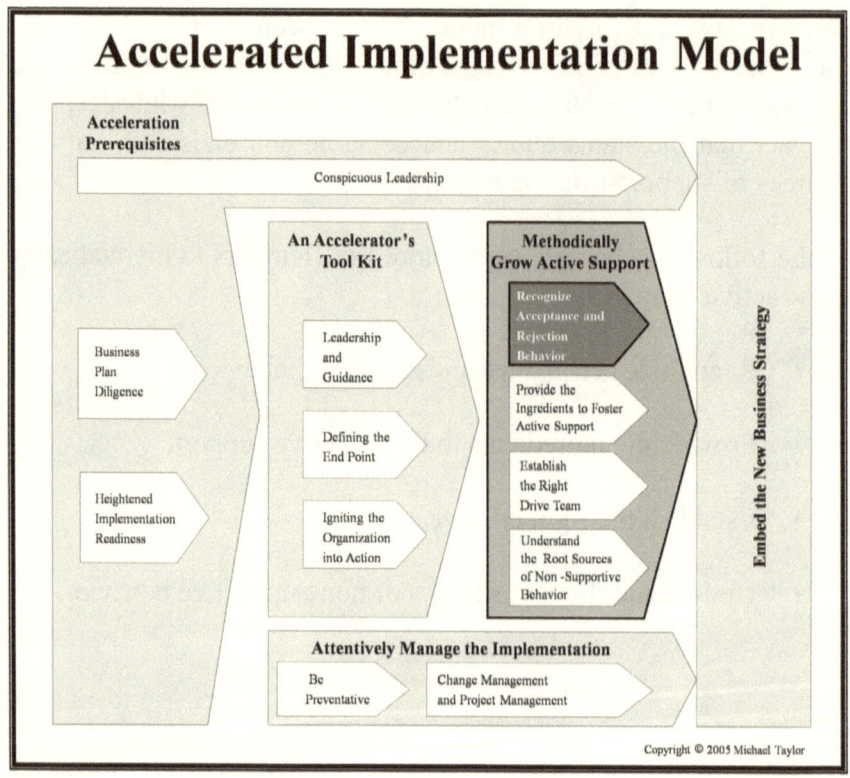

Accelerated Implementation Model

Acceleration Prerequisites

Conspicuous Leadership

An Accelerator's Tool Kit

Methodically Grow Active Support

Business Plan Diligence

Leadership and Guidance

Recognize Acceptance and Rejection Behavior

Defining the End Point

Provide the Ingredients to Foster Active Support

Heightened Implementation Readiness

Igniting the Organization into Action

Establish the Right Drive Team

Understand the Root Sources of Non -Supportive Behavior

Embed the New Business Strategy

Attentively Manage the Implementation

Be Preventative

Change Management and Project Management

Recognize That People Differ

As mentioned in earlier chapters, each individual goes through his or her own individual stages of adoption of new business initiatives. Everyone accepts or rejects, adopts or rebuffs new ideas at their own pace. The successful leader who wants to accelerate business-strategy implementation recognizes that people differ, understands the acceptance process, and enacts the right ingredients of talent and tools to win acceptance and then generate active support; first the support of a core group of people and then quickly a growing critical mass of people.

People differ. Given the identical information, two individuals will not accept a new idea to the same degree or adopt a new activity at the same rate. Some people thrive in change and enthusiastically look for challenges. These people embrace new things quickly. Others are naturally cautious and are inclined to be reluctant until they fully understand the "new way." These people are apt to wait until it is proven that the "new way" is better than the existing way. Therefore it is important to do more than just outline the logical merits of the new business strategy. It is important to recognize that the adoption process will not progress at a uniform pace throughout a group of people. If we recognize the differences of individuals, we can still help the adoption process along and even accelerate it.

Even though you explain the shortcomings of the status quo, explain the merits of the new business strategy, and describe a Compelling Attraction to reduce anxiety and create a new comfort zone, people will adopt and support or reject the new business strategy to varying degrees and at different rates. Somewhat like the widely known pattern of technology adoption, there are typical categories of response behavior when a new business idea or a major change is introduced. Typically, after the announcement and explanation of a new business strategy or a major initiative, response behaviors fall into a range of types from the enthusiastic participants to the reluctant pragmatists to the skeptics and the objectors.

Typical Response Behavior Types

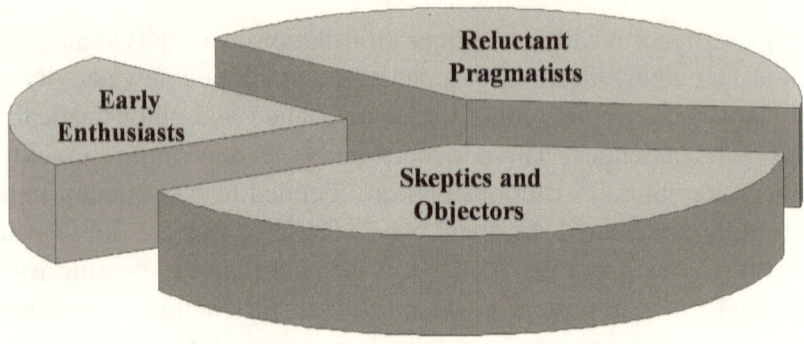

Like adopting a new technology, a new business strategy or initiative can affect an individual's job function, work assignment, work environment, and most delicate of all, sometimes a person's perceived ability to be successful. On an individual basis, business changes can have a major impact on a person's work life and, for that individual, put a lot more at risk than is understood by the change leaders. If you are in doubt of this point, just visit any major bookstore and review the business books outlining failures of CRM (customer-relationship management) systems. For the most part the technology was not the hurdle. The major hurdle was the acceptance, or more accurately the lack of acceptance, of the need for the new system and the change to work habits that was required for the new system to become workable.

It is helpful to have a few enthusiasts in your organization. These are usually those people who are comfortable in an abstract unstructured environment, those who like to try new things, those who are adventurous, and/or those who don't worry about the consequences of failure. Early enthusiasts can play a key role in your core drive team, but be careful—some enthusiasts may not have the credibility to be a drive team leader. Enthusiasts often lack credibility with doubting audiences in the organization, since they may be seen as someone who falls in love with every new idea or is too carefree, blindly optimistic, fickle, reckless, and not thinking through the consequences of proposed new ideas. Sometimes these are the people who are enthusiastic because they have the most to gain from the change or they are the ones who have been "waiting for this to happen." The energy and enthusiasm these individuals offer can be a major asset to the drive team. A final word of caution about early enthusiasts—evaluate the depth of an enthusiast's commitment before putting them in any kind of leadership role. Shallow enthusiasts can become passionate about another idea next week, and the enthusiasm for your initiative can evaporate as quickly as it appeared.

Reluctant pragmatists are those who want to see it working before jumping on the "bandwagon." Sometimes they are reluctant to let go of the old established ways, being not comfortable with change, and must be shown how the new system works. The Compelling Attraction and a detailed explanation of the implementation road map are helpful with this group of people. Some cautious individuals like to run parallel systems for a long time to take some of the risk out of the adoption process. On the positive side, when pragmatists become committed to your new strategy, they usually provide solid support and can be good allies to grow support for the new business approach.

Skeptics and objectors are slower adopters, and some will never adopt. Skeptics don't believe in the new business strategy and often believe that the status quo is just fine, despite risks and shortcomings. Some skeptics accept the need for change but doubt that the new ideas will work. Their objections may, to some degree, be valid, and they may identify critical problems that will face the implementation drive team. On the other hand, they may just not like change. In the critical early stages of implementation, you need to get as much adoption acceleration as possible to build a critical mass of support. When it comes to skeptics who are in leadership roles in the organization, weigh how much effort you want to invest in these people. An exhaustive amount of time may still not encourage adoption.

Occasionally you will find people who absolutely object to the new business strategy for a number of reasons, perhaps because the new business strategy is out of sync with their capabilities, their career goals, their work environment necessities, their values, or their morals. (See the later chapter on root sources of resistance to find possible causes for such strong resistance.) These people sometimes feel so strongly against the new business strategy that they will never buy in. They may quit or, worse, stay and become potential saboteurs. You may have to take some dramatic action. Their influence must be minimized by isolating them or by removing them from the organization.

As we mentioned at the outset, each individual goes through his or her own individual process of adoption. We can generalize a little to identify typical response behavior and group people in categories. However, we cannot lose sight of the fact that individuals are unique and everyone behaves, accepts, rejects, adopts, or rebuffs new ideas in their own style.

The Adoption/Rejection Process

A Process, Not an Instantaneous Change

Let's go back to the enthusiasts and the reluctant pragmatists for a minute. Every person, regardless of his or her inclination for one type of adoption behavior or another, goes through an adoption or rejection process.

People do not switch from their current norms to new practices instantaneously. As we have mentioned earlier, most people go through a process that starts with accepting the fact that the status quo is unacceptable and ends with varying degrees of support or opposition. Support can vary from those who are strong advocates of the new plan and who help drive accelerated adoption to those who are entrenched opponents of the new plan and who might recruit cohorts. During the process, each individual goes through his or her own individual stages of acceptance and/or rejection. Each individual will adopt or rebuff at his or her own rate. In addition to employing the best ingredients, talent, and tools to win acceptance and generate active support, the successful leader who wants to accelerate the implementation of a new business initiative must recognize that people differ and must understand the acceptance process. The process of winning support is a series of steps building on one another. The steps are a gradual process of understanding, acceptance, and support. Support for your new ideas can grow and create strong advocates in the organization who can help accelerate your implementation plans. On the other hand, objections, reluctance, and anxiety can diminish, delay, or evaporate support and slow your implementation plans. The chart on the following page outlines some of the potential phases during this Adoption/Rejection Process.

The Adoption/Rejection Process steps can be viewed in three phases: the Awareness Phase, the Fluid Transition Phase, and the Entrenchment Phase. The awareness phase is the easiest to understand and to accomplish. This is the phase of launch announcements that were discussed in the earlier chapter about the Igniting Event. Implementation challenges start to become evident when people in the organization start to understand the impact of your announcements and plans in the fluid transition phase.

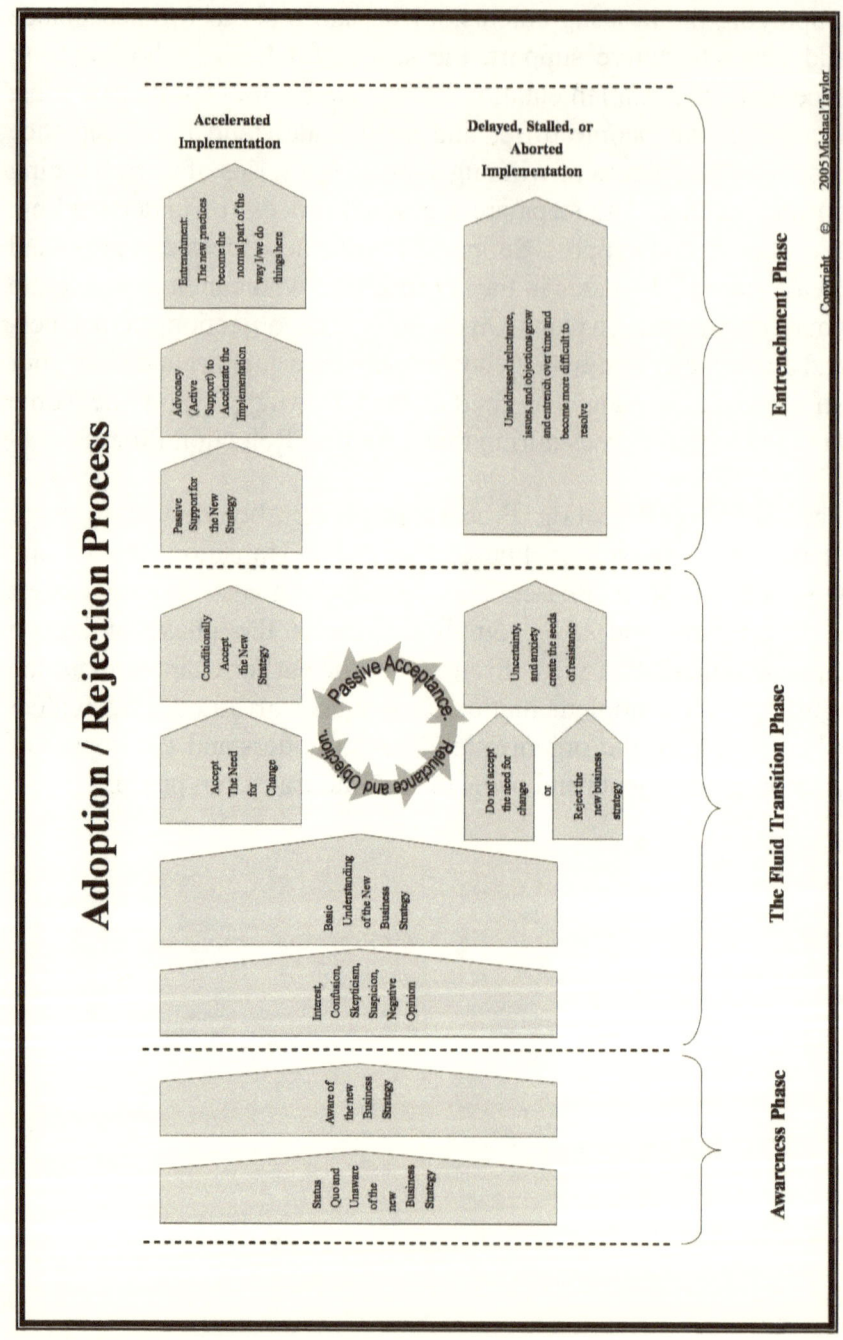

The Fluid Transition Phase

The most vulnerable phase of the Adoption/Rejection Process is in the transition to initial acceptance or rejection. I refer to this as the fluid transition phase. The words "fluid" and "transition" aptly describe the behavior in this stage. During this phase, people *transition* from the stage of simply being aware of your new plans to the stage of entrenched positions of either supporting or opposing the new plans. This stage is *fluid* because, as people learn more and understand the impact of the new plans, they often flip-flop from passive support to reluctance and objection while they come to terms individually and make a personal assessment of the situation. At the end of the fluid transition phase, commonly each individual will have developed a mind-set that either supports or opposes your new plans. Let's take a closer look at what happens in this phase so you can influence and grow support for your new ideas.

Typically, every individual, upon learning of a new idea, has some initial confusion or suspicion and a healthy balance of trust and skepticism. Everyone, including managers at all levels, should have a cautious curiosity about new ideas. This is all normal. In most organizations, the initial reactions of most people to business changes include a healthy interest in the business, a healthy bit of skepticism about new ideas, and a healthy appetite for more information so they can understand the new ideas being presented.

At this early point, each person forms what he or she believes is a rational opinion. This rational judgment determines if the new business plan is a positive or a negative move for the business *and* for them personally. At this step in the Adoption/Rejection Process, he or she starts to form an opinion about whether the new plan is favorable or not. In these early stages, favorable is, at best, conditional support for your new plans, as they understand more about the impact of the changes ahead. An unfavorable assessment may be the result of anxiety associated with change or may simply be the normal response of a skeptical person while they gather information and understand the impact of the new ideas.

In this early fluid time, we want to do our best to minimize any confusion. Initial reactions of confusion usually create anxiety and almost always create negative opinions of a new business strategy, even with the most resilient people. As we will discuss in a later section, anxiety and objections can emerge for a variety of reasons, confusion being a big one.

This first assessment can become entrenched quickly and can be hard to reverse, so it is important to communicate a powerful and convincing message at the outset. There are two key points here: First, follow through with your communication of the 100-Second Enlightenment and the Compelling Attraction. Second, and equally as important, listen and allow people to air their opinions. Accept that those opinions are genuine to the individual expressing them. Explore the root causes of reluctance or objections. Clarify any confusion immediately and indicate how other problems will be explored further. More on this later.

Although pragmatists and skeptics may, in due time, accept the new business strategy, they should be considered conscientious protesters who need to have their concerns heard. At a minimum you can provide the ingredients for clear understanding, listen to objections, provide clarification, answer questions, and help resolve issues, and hopefully a consensus of support will grow. The reasons supporting the need for a new business approach, the Compelling Attraction, and the 100-Second Enlightenment will be very useful for the leaders in the organization as well as the people in the organization—the deliverers and receivers of the message.

For some early enthusiasts, the transition from awareness to support can be relatively quick. The speed of the transition is largely dependent on how dramatic the shift is in business strategy, on how dramatic the personal impact is on the people, and on how accustomed or receptive the organization is to change. Even the most dynamic organizational cultures can grind to a halt while each individual takes the time to understand the impact of the changes.

Your people are most at risk during the fluid transition phase. This is when they are the least productive, there is more "watercooler chitchat," and small groups debate the merits and risks of the proposed ideas. There may be concerns about job security, career disruption, loss of position or influence, and many other factors. There is often an upturn in personal Internet surfing to find out more information. This is also a time when your top talent pool is most vulnerable to competitive raiding. A raid on your most talented people is sometimes hard to defend after you launch a major business initiative. While you are embroiled in internal changes, the turmoil of transition, and the attention required by your launch activities, you have little time left to deal with a competitive threat. The best thing you can do to combat these issues is to be engaged with the people in your organization as much as possible. See the chapter "Conspicuous Leadership."

The Entrenchment Phase

There is no point in time marking the end of the fluid transition phase. Suddenly you will realize that there is a critical mass of people in the organization who are passively or actively supporting the new game plan. Once someone accepts a new idea, typically they pass through phases of conditional support while they learn and understand more, to passive support; and a few people become active supporters who develop into advocates for the new strategy. Once you have a critical mass of support, you are in the entrenchment phase and you have two parallel focal activities.

First, there will always be a few holdouts who refuse to support the new initiatives or openly oppose them. Don't write off the holdouts. These are not troublemakers. They are people who are reluctant to support or have objections to the new initiatives. Likely they have skills, experience, and talent that you will need. They may have unaddressed objections or problems that they need help to solve. Unaddressed objections and concerns become entrenched over time and become more difficult to resolve. Unaddressed objections and concerns act like putting the brakes on to slow down your accelerated implementation plans. See the chapter "Understanding the Root Causes of Non-Supporting Behavior."

Second, focus a growing part of your attention on strengthening passive support into advocacy and growing the number of active supporters. Support grows over time with encouragement, with resolution of objections, with reassurance in the new strategy, and with evidence of success. A growing advocacy of the new strategy will greatly accelerate when a critical mass of people, maybe one-third or more, embrace the new strategy and evidence of early success becomes well-known in the organization. As the critical mass of supporters grows, more and more doubting pragmatists come on board. The skeptics and objectors will soon be the outsiders, and the new strategy will become the normal way of conducting business. Usually this growing support is the result of a lot of work to resolve the objectionable issues, a lot of coaching at the grassroots level, and the introduction of enabling infrastructure to allow easy change to new processes and job functions and time to accept the new ideas.

As we have discussed, the adoption and/or rejection is a process that each individual in the organization must go through. In most cases you cannot coach every single employee, but you can be prepared to listen and address concerns and provide ingredients such as descriptions of the Compelling Attractions. You can start with a core drive team to help multiply the number of "message carriers" and "objection resolvers." Recognizing the adoption process helps us facilitate it and allows us to get through the fluid transition phase as quickly and successfully as possible to develop a critical mass of supporters and the resulting accelerated implementation of the new business plans.

A Few Key Points, from Experience, to Help the Adoption Process

Acceptance and Adoption Take Time; We Are Dealing with People, Not Machines

As leaders in the organization, it is often difficult to balance the need to be aggressive with the need to be patient and realistic with your people. As mentioned previously, people must be given time to understand the changes that will result from the new business strategy before they accept it. Granted, there are often early enthusiasts who will get on board fairly quickly, but the majority of people will need some time. It takes time to think through, understand, consider the information and alternatives, and finally accept the need for change, the merits of the new business strategy, and the validity of the end point the organization is being asked to work toward.

Some People Do Not Adopt Change Easily; Help Them

There is a process of adoption that every affected person goes through. Recognize it and help your people through it. Review the description of the Compelling Attraction and explain how it will impact those people individually. Provide reassurance and communicate progress so they can see the light at the end of the tunnel. It is important for many people to know that the turmoil of transition is temporary. Reiterate the stability and the detailed picture of the end point that you are working toward. They will start to see the pieces of the change taking place and recognize that the transition is progressing.

Very few people can cope continuously in a state of turmoil. It is best to have as short a transition period as possible. Usually short transition periods require more preparation and have more upfront expenses, but this is offset by the shorter loss of productivity and financial results.

During the early announcements and implementation, there will be challenges and obstacles identified. Individuals will not be able to solve all of them. No doubt some will be small local departmental issues that are not a priority. The implementation drive team will have to keep an eye out for small issues that frontline teams need help to resolve. Try to make help available quickly. This will help reduce the anxiety if frontline people know they will not be abandoned and left to implement this new strategy on their own.

Build a Growing Acceptance of New Ideas before Implementing Them

Make sure you have growing acceptance of your initiative or new business strategy before moving on to implementation. If people feel they are being run over by changes, it can give them a sense of no control and of being a victim. You risk creating unnecessary resistance by starting the implementation without an acceptance period. Changing processes and job functions with a group of people who do not understand the new strategy or who have not accepted the need for change will only create anxiety.

Build around Your Supporters to Accelerate Acceptance

Build around your supporters and win over influential and opinion leaders. Local grassroots supporters have local credibility with their peers since they are perceived as understanding the local conditions and practical requirements. This has even more impact if the local supporter is already an influential opinion leader. Assist your local supporters. Give local supporters access to information and the implementation drive team. This will not only accelerate acceptance but will also provide valuable feedback from the front line. Local supporters can help late adopters (pragmatists and skeptics) by providing clarification and answering questions in a friendly environment. Local supporters can also provide feedback to the implementation drive team that will help make the rollout less disruptive on the front line.

Some People Will Not Survive; Get Over This Early

As mentioned in earlier sections, the new business strategy may result in changes that require some people to lose positions or be dismissed. There are a number of reasons for people to move to other positions or leave the organization. There may be a mismatch with the new skill requirements, they may be a disruptive objector to the new strategy, or they may not want to stay in the organization under the new plan. If people changes are required, get through this as early as possible. People changes are always a shock to any organization. If people need to be dismissed, it is important to get this done early so the people remaining in the organization know that the changes are over and they can stop worrying about their own employment. While people are worried about their own job security, they will not be productive or actively support any new ideas. The best thing is to get through this stage as early as possible and announce it is over.

Don't Forget, You Were Skeptical at First Too

Managers often hear announcements before the rest of the people in the organization, and these same managers often forget their own initial reluctance and make a common misjudgment. At some later date when they are presenting the new business strategy to their group, they forget their own initial reactions to the new business strategy and expect immediate excitement from their people. These same managers are now way down the adoption process and must allow their employees time to work through these normal feelings and reactions to the new ideas being presented to them.

Executives Can Easily Lose Sight of Implementation Progress

It is easy for executives to assume that the new strategy is implemented and the change is over before it really has taken root. They are often early enthusiasts and fast adopters themselves. To them it seems like they communicated the vision a long time ago, but it takes time to filter down to the people who will actually have to change their behavior.

When an executive parachutes into a frontline office or a shop-floor department and meets someone who is still trying to understand the new plan and is just getting on board with the new program, it may seem to the visiting executive like the organization is rebelling and not adopting the change. In fact, it may be that it has taken a long time to get the specifics of the plan defined and communication done.

Some executives focus on the progress of the rollout stage. As part of the implementation rollout, quite often people in the organization are asked to develop new processes, tools, and procedures, even though they are still (at least partially) carrying out their existing job responsibilities. It takes time to get all these things done.

Chapter 8

Provide the Ingredients to Foster Active Support

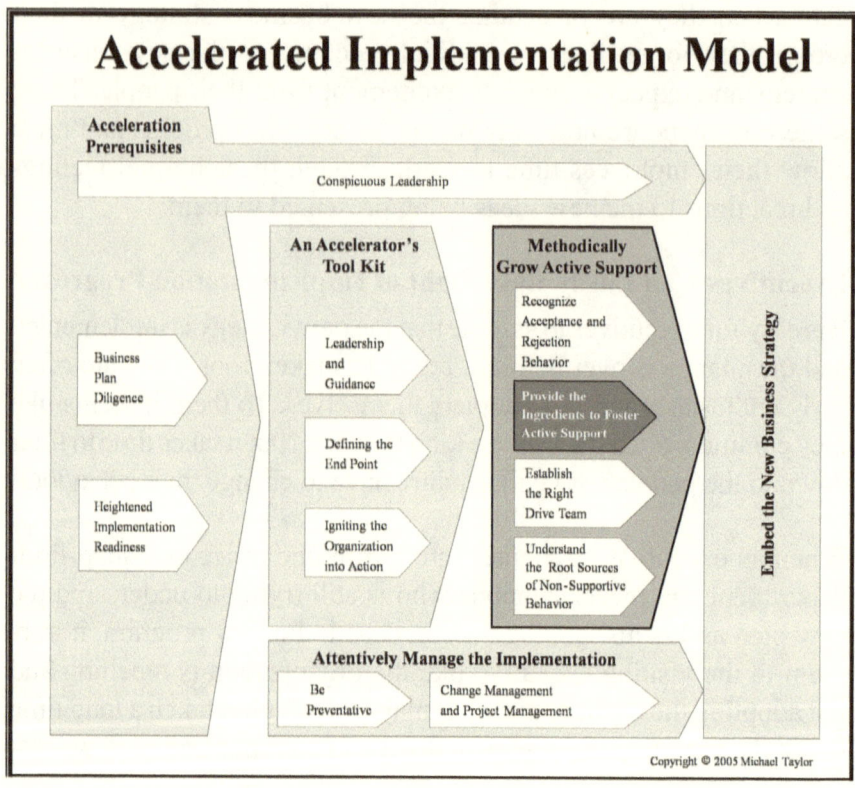

Accelerated Implementation Model

Copyright © 2005 Michael Taylor

The Right Ingredients Improve the Probability of Success

Rapidly creating active support and enthusiasm for the new business initiatives is our goal. To accelerate the implementation of new business initiatives, you need to accelerate the adoption process and create as many enthusiasts as possible. As we have discussed in pervious sections, we need to encourage each affected individual in the organization and present them with the following expectations:

- Accept the need to change or the need for a new strategy.

- Become confident that the new business strategy will be successful.

- Grow that confidence so that each individual will actively support and accelerate the implementation of the new business plan.

The ingredients and tips I describe in the following few pages will not resolve all potential pitfalls, but they will help individuals go through their personal process of acceptance with a faster adoption rate and a higher likelihood of coming out in support of the new strategy at the end of the fluid transition phase discussed in the previous chapter.

Once individuals start to accept the new strategy, active support is not instantaneous nor guaranteed. People will advance through the process of accepting the new ideas and move on to supporting the new ideas. The various topics of this chapter outline the ingredients to grow a strong foundation to build, first, passive support, and then strong active support. As you have already seen, there are no shortcuts and no sure bets. Successfully accelerating the implementation of your new business strategy is a matter of stacking the odds in your favor with as many positive ingredients as possible.

Accepting the Need to Change

Senior managers too often assume that it must be obvious to the people in the organization that we are not being successful. Senior managers assume that those people will recognize the need for change. This is a dangerous assumption. Even when individuals realize that the organization is not meeting profit targets, they quite often believe that their own group is performing fine and conclude that it must be some other part of the organization or a systemic issue. The first hurdle in accelerating the implementation of a new business strategy is to get individuals to accept that the status quo is not acceptable.

Note: This disconnect between management views and the perception of frontline operations' people is more prevalent in large organizations where communication is often lost in layers of management or individual groups are operating as islands of information.

Sometimes the common opinion is "What's wrong with leaving it the way it is—we are doing okay. It ain't broke, so why are we going to change the way we run the business and screw things up? The current approach is a tried-and-true method that we have fine-tuned for years. Let's leave things just the way they are." Your first big task is to explain why the status quo is not acceptable. The second big task is to get people to accept this as reality. This often takes an explanation of your research, an opportunity for people to have their questions answered, and enough time for individuals to digest and accept your message.

Prepare to present a compelling reason to change. Successful explanations have the following elements:

- specific reasons and facts, not generalities

- a description of the business forces driving the change

- reference to the diligence in the research and analysis to build credibility

- an honest assessment of the urgency

- a projection of the outcomes of the status quo

The explanation should be as specific as possible and not abstract. For example, it is not very effective to say, "We are introducing a new information-management system because the existing one does not provide the output necessary to manage the company." It is more effective to explain that "the existing system does not provide detailed real-time information on the status of customer orders, which is necessary for us to comply with our customers' requirements." If possible be even more specific; for example, "Our competitor has a market share of X percent and a Y percent on-time delivery rate. We need to implement this new system to pinpoint areas we need to improve to help us exceed Y percent on-time delivery. If we do not improve our delivery performance, our business is expected to drop by Z percent and we will face downsizing."

Explain the business forces driving the need for change. Your diligent research and analysis has led you to this point where you feel a change to your business approach is necessary. Share this with the people in the organization as much as you can. There may be some proprietary or competitive information that you do not want to broadcast, but try to give everyone as complete an understanding as possible. The credibility of your explanation will take a big boost if your people can see it is the result of solid research and analysis. The clear message must show a link between the business forces and the need for a change. It must be clear that the new strategy is not just a reason for you to boost your career or to make a change simply to show your superiors that you are doing something, or anything. Explain the link to the business forces driving the need for change. Perhaps you are reacting to market or competitive pressures or anticipating technology developments or regulatory changes. The research detailing the pressures that are driving the change in business strategy will help develop credibility in your explanation.

Be honest about the urgency of the situation. It will not take long for everyone to see the reality, and if you have tried to paint a false picture of impending doom, the credibility for all other elements of the new strategy will diminish. Be honest: Is this an urgent crisis, such as facing insolvency or the loss of a major contract or customer? Is there a competitive deadline, such as a competitor expected to launch a new product in the second fiscal quarter? Is there a market deadline, such as the annual industry exhibition? Perhaps the shareholders are expecting the organization to surpass a certain milestone by the end of the year.

What will be the outcome if you do nothing? A projection of the outcomes of the status quo is not a point to dwell on, but it will be a question everyone will be asking. All change has a cost—is this new business strategy going to be worth the effort and the opportunity cost of the status quo? As part of your analysis, you have projected the expected results of the status quo. Share this with your people. You may also have some early estimates of the cost of implementation or the cost change—share these too. The situation of the status quo must be clear to build credibility in the need for change.

Developing and Growing Confidence in the New Strategy

Once you have explained why the current situation is unacceptable and why a new business strategy is necessary, the next steps are to gain acceptance, followed by support, then active support, and ultimately (hopefully) enthusiasm for the new strategy. The people in your organization must have the confidence that the new strategy will be more successful than the status quo. Outline your Compelling Attraction. If the people in the organization accept the need for change, then your challenge is to develop confidence in the new business strategy and the organization's ability to make it a success. There are a number of key elements that should be included in your arguments:

- A reference to the level of diligence that went into the research and the analysis to build credibility into your arguments that follow.

- The alternatives that you included in your evaluation and a short description of pros and cons of each and why the selected alternative is the best.

- A description of the Compelling Attraction—the mind's-eye picture described in earlier chapters. This description should be sufficiently detailed to allow your audience to picture the responsibilities of individual roles and positions, to picture how key processes will change, and to understand the benefits, how improved results will be generated.

- An explanation of how this new business strategy is in line with the overall vision and long-term goals for the business.

- A summary of the expected implementation strategy. Describe a compelling journey of how the organization will develop the Compelling Attraction into reality. Perhaps the rollout will be in phases or with certain target groups in the organization. Answer questions like who will lead the implementation, will there be an implementation team or a steering committee, will people be assigned full-time to the rollout project, will the organization structure change during the implementation, and what are the expected duration of the implementation and the expected performance milestones. Punctuate your implementation explanation with the priorities, the urgent items, and the key deliverables that will define success.

- An explanation of how people will be able to ask questions, get clarification, provide feedback, have input into the development of the new plans, and get involved in their area.

- A description of the resources, budget, people, and training that have been designated for the implementation of the new business strategy.

- A summary of the management plan in place to demonstrate commitment and confirm the credibility of the management team's ability to successfully implement the new strategy. This normally includes a commitment of personal involvement by the leadership team, a performance-measurement and reward system, and a performance- or progress-review process. Involvement of key senior players in the leadership team and not the assistant who "speaks on behalf of the management team" will be perceived as a real sign of the management's commitment to the new strategy.

Support is not instantaneous. People take time to internalize and believe in something. The larger the change expected from the status quo, the longer the time the acceptance will take. If the change is inconsistent with the corporate culture, described by some as "the way we do things around here," then the acceptance time will be longer and there will be more likelihood that there will be deep-rooted resistance.

Accelerating into Active Support

Active support is not a natural progression from acceptance. We need to encourage passive supporters to become active supporters. The most effective accelerating technique is to create a growing team that is motivated to implement the new strategy and consequently become active supporters of the implementation plan. A small team of enthusiasts can be contagious and grow into a critical mass of active supporters in the organization.

Fortunately, there are often a few people in any group whose personal style is to lead. Often these individuals not only feel a need to be in a leadership role but also feel a need to have an impact and to make a difference. In most cases, however, there are not enough of these assertive supporters to grow a critical mass of support by themselves. You will need to motivate more active supporters until the active supporters become a critical mass within the organization and the non-supporters are a minority.

A few things need to be in place to help people cast off old methods and become active participants in implementation activities of the new business strategy:

- It must be low risk for them, with no worries about loss of position or career opportunity.

- The performance-measurement system, reward system, and incentive plans must not penalize supporters who stop doing things "the old way."

- There needs to be a sense of urgency to implement the new plan, with milestones and deadlines.

- Finally, there needs to be an igniting kickoff event to plan and organize initial implementation efforts and most importantly to generate the energy to detonate the drive team into action.

Naturally these active supporters need some structure and organization to be effective. This is the task of the drive team that is described in the next chapter.

Once the active support begins, communicate those efforts and the progress. Openly acknowledge and recognize the efforts of the active supporters and their progress. This sends a message to the organization about the expectations of the desired way we do things here. The best ingredient to help accelerate the implementation of your new business strategy is a growing group of enthusiasts who actively drive the implementation plans and create a culture that envelops the new strategy.

A Few Points, from Experience, about Growing Support

Accelerated Implementation ≠ Immediate Impact; Change Takes Time

Unlike a project where there is a start and a completion, implementing a new business strategy has a lingering effect. The new business strategy is not a onetime event; it is a permanent change. Major strategy shifts mean processes will change, structures will change, and roles and responsibilities will change, and this often will affect everyone in the organization to some degree. There can be no bystanders or nonparticipants. Sooner or later everyone in the affected groups will be impacted by the strategy change.

Widespread change takes time and cannot happen at one "switch-over" point, even though the culmination of the change may be a launch date where much of the "switch-over" occurs. This is common for initiatives such as the acquisition of one firm by another or the launch of an enterprise-wide software platform. The switch-over of major systems will necessarily happen on an enterprise-wide basis, but this is the finale of a long change-preparation period and often the midpoint of the impact of the new initiative.

Build Support at Each Level of Management

Managers need to understand new ideas before they can stand in front of the ideas and communicate them to their employees or customers. There is a process of understanding new concepts, internalizing/digesting/becoming familiar with the details, and assuming each manager agrees with the ideas and get their questions answered, ultimately they can become confident with the ideas. This occurs at each level. Also, the process gets more granular as you get closer to those who will be directly impacted by the change and the people who will be experiencing process or job changes. The more granular the issues, the more time it takes to work through the acceptance process.

Balance Participation and Acceleration

Involvement is a question of balance. It would be pleasantly utopian to have everyone involved in the planning process and give everyone a chance to contribute and feel some ownership of the new business strategy. This extreme is anything but accelerated. On the other hand, it is sometimes a little shocking to have a strategy implemented from the ivory tower of a head office with no involvement from the people in the organization. This extreme is ripe for plenty of resistance, perhaps to the point of losing key people or the point of sabotage. What is the best answer—slow democracy or expedient dictatorship? Involving your people is a balance between participation and acceleration.

Since the new strategy needs to become part of the culture of "the way we do things here" and have an impact on the people and their effectiveness long after the new business-strategy implementation is complete, it is important that the people in the organization feel some ownership for success. So it is important to include them in various ways:

- Get them involved as early as possible.

- Give them some power to mold the tactical details of the new strategy.

- Since few plans are perfect or detailed in the first planning session, give selected people in the organization some power to influence the leadership and design the tactical elements of the strategy and business plans.

- Ask them to help solve problems and design measurement systems.

- Employ people from the affected groups to become members of the drive team.

Participation costs time. It is good to develop a sense of ownership and include people in the organization to plan the tactical aspects of the plan, but opening up the overall implementation planning for discussion is a slippery slope. Limit planning to key stakeholders and fix them to a short deadline to define a recommended implementation solution. By opening up the implementation planning for discussion, you have started your accelerated implementation with a planning delay. Any planning team should be given rigid expectations and scope. The one thing you want to avoid is to plant the seeds of delay by implying that everything may be open for debate.

Repeat, Repeat, Repeat—Articulate the Benefits Often
You cannot repeat the benefits of the new strategy often enough. Remember that we are creating purpose for your people. People in the organization will repeatedly ask themselves why were are doing this; for what benefit? Their daily hurdles will remind them of the difficulty caused by the new business strategy, so they need to be reminded often of the benefits—both for the business and for the individuals in the organization.

This activity does more than any other to reduce resistance later. Make sure all affected groups are included when identifying the benefits. Be as specific as possible. Personalize the benefits as much as possible to make sure individuals understand the benefits individually. Emphasize how an individual or a group has an impact on the success of the organization. Don't underestimate the importance of the business organization. Most people have a desire to be part of something successful. Point out the success—the benefits—that the business is expected to experience. Remind them not only why this new business strategy is good, but also why the new business strategy is better than the old strategy.

Be Direct and Open about the Impact of the New Business Strategy

Your benefits message should be realistic. Don't overpromise—this will reduce the credibility of your arguments. Similarly, don't hide any negative aspects. Point out the implementation challenges; your message will have a lot more credibility if you can demonstrate that you have thought through the process and have identified the challenges that lie ahead as well as the benefits. For the same reasons of credibility, it is important to identify the challenges on the personal front and the things that will be lost.

- Identify who will be impacted and point out the support that will be provided.

- Listen to the feedback and opposition, because it may be telling you that you have not identified all the groups that will be impacted or that there are critical obstacles that need to be considered or managed.

- In each impacted group, gain their acceptance for the need for change. Then get their acceptance of the new business model.

- Identify and segment the target audiences. Do your impact analysis on each group. Create a communication plan for each group. This allows you to effectively flavor the communications to each group, to better foresee potential resistance, and to better handle resistance rather than rely on a common vanilla approach to all. In the end, segmenting will prepare the drive team to more effectively target and customize training. "Flavoring" the message for different segment groups must be limited to changing the emphasis of parts of the message. The primary messages to all groups must be the same or you risk the organization sensing that untruths are being communicated and something underhanded is about to happen.

This will create a better plan, prepare the organization for the changes to come, and initiate the early adopters into action. If the change will threaten some people and you expect a significant backlash, work disruption, or sabotage, then prepare to mitigate this risk immediately upon the announcements—but don't hide the news.

Be honest, direct, and open about the impact and changes that will be caused by the new business strategy. This will develop credibility in the message and ultimately will develop credibility in any later information that follows. At the same time you can begin to set the expectations for progress and success.

It Isn't as Obvious as You May Think

A common mistake is to assume that the merit in the business plan is obvious to everyone and that they will automatically be as supportive as you are. This dangerous assumption can create the seeds of resistance. When you are explaining the new business strategy or why the existing strategy is unacceptable or the details of the Compelling Attraction or the 100-Second Enlightenment, don't fall into the trap of thinking the conclusions are obvious. It may be obvious to you, but you have been living with the idea for some time; the ideas in the new business strategy are new to the receiving audience. In addition, senior managers and change leaders often have a predisposition to early adoption and are open-minded and comfortable in abstract situations. Not everyone else has these traits. Consequently, what may seem obvious to you may seem unclear or a roadblock to others. Take the time to comprehensively explain every step and ask questions to test if the message is clear.

The Front Line Can Uncover Hidden Complexity

Don't underestimate the complexity of the new business strategy or time required to understand the new approach. As a business leader, you have more experience analyzing and understanding complex situations. If the new business initiatives are complicated, people in your organization may struggle a little to understand some of the new ideas. Consider this in your messaging and allow time for questions and discussion.

As your new business-strategy message reaches the front line of the organization—those who will be directly impacted by the change or the people who will be experiencing process or job changes—the questions and the discussion get more granular. It is only at the most granular levels that the real complexity sometimes becomes apparent. Sometimes this is where new issues become evident, such as logistical constraints, material shortages, specialized skill requirements, facility limitations, and many more possibilities. It is only at this stage in the rollout that portions of the implementation plan that you thought were going to be straightforward become complicated and create delays in your accelerated plans.

There Are Many Interpretations of the New Business Strategy

Even though everyone may agree with the concept, they may be interpreting and visualizing a different solution and making different underlying and unspoken assumptions. Often, the outcome of the new business strategy isn't as obvious as you think. This applies to senior executives as well as to frontline employees.

After articulating the need for change and the new business strategy, the best clarifying tool is often a description of the end point; that is, the Compelling Attraction. It may be inappropriate to get too granular at early announcements, but it is important to follow up and get more granular in answering questions. First you want to get people to buy into the concept. It is important to recognize that fairly early in the adoption process everyone starts to visualize how it will work on the ground. This is where their own bias or their own interpretation will determine their own "on the ground vision." You may say that this can be straightened out later, but managers will use their interpreted version to answer questions from their staff. You can avoid a lot of clarification and refocusing effort later by painting a detailed picture early. Everyone will interpret messages and ideas based on their own personal experience and set of values, but you can reduce the spectrum of those interpretations with the detailed mind's-eye description of the Compelling Attraction.

Several years ago I was involved in introducing a matrix organization to one of the functional areas of a large industrial firm. The organizational concept seemed straightforward. The reporting structure was defined, job descriptions were clear, and the performance-measurement system was thought out, but the perceived complexity was underestimated. The people who would now be part of the new matrix organization understood the concept of a matrix organization, but as became clear later, they each interpreted the new business approach and the on-the-ground impact a little differently. They each had their own interpretation of how they would do their daily work, report their progress, and have their performance measured. Follow-up communication and more detailed descriptions helped many people. In the end there were still a few people who needed to experience the new system being demonstrated so they understood how it would work at the ground level.

Repeat the Message from the Frontline Managers

Ultimately every affected person in the organization must have a working understanding of the new business strategy. I say a "working understanding" because not everyone needs to know the intricate details of, for instance, technology, financial, or logistical matters. However, in order for individuals to support a new idea, they must first understand it and believe it. This is why the frontline managers and supervisors are an important part of the communication plan. Front-line managers and supervisors can fulfill several needs to improve employees understanding and substantiate the credibility of the message.

Frontline managers and supervisors usually have credibility with the people who report to them since they understand the local situation and can put the new business strategy in the context of the local team. Frontline management can flavor the message to include the dimension "what this means for us in our department or location." Flavoring can reduce anxiety associated with change and unknown consequences and add credibility to the executive message that all employees may have already heard. The assumption often made is … if the executives and my own manager are on the same page and on board, then the message has credibility.

Unfortunately, "flavoring" can also result in message drift, which can cause all kinds of problems if people believe they understand the new strategy only to hear a different game plan, the accurate one, later. Often there are several layers of management between the executive team, with the original message, and the frontline management. It is important to make sure the message has not drifted from its original meaning and content.

Remember the childhood telephone game that had a bunch of kids sit in a circle. The first child whispered a message to the next, who in turn whispered it to the next, until the last child said the message out loud. The first child then repeated the original message out loud and all the children had fun listening to the difference between the original version and the final version of the message. This can happen with adults as well. As a message travels through several layers of management, the content of the original message can drift. To avoid message drift, it is helpful for frontline managers to hear the message directly from the executive team.

"In-person" executive briefing sessions with frontline management are the most effective method to give this key group of people an accurate message to carry forward to their people. This also allows these important influencers, the frontline management, to ask questions, to hear the passion in the executive's voice, to sense the commitment of the executive team, to assess the credibility of the plan, and to evaluate the capability of the leadership team to be successful. This can have a major impact in the tone used by the front-line managers when they convey the message and answer questions with their report line.

Although live "in-person" communication is more expensive than sending out e-mail or distributing a management circular, these sessions can have a dramatic impact on the early acceleration of your business-strategy implementation. It is usually worth the expense.

Two-Way Communication—Listen for Valid Criticism

Face time between executives and employees is always a positive step to improve understanding of the new business strategy and to motivate support. Employee town hall meetings and employee roundtable discussions are excellent approaches for management at all levels to explain a new business strategy.

Use these sessions as early as possible as forums to repeat the 100-Second Enlightenment, to communicate the Compelling Attraction, and to outline the implementation road map. The first few forums can be used to test and fine-tune the message approach. Use the questions raised to improve the delivery of the message at the next session.

Equally as important as communicating your message is to listen for and gauge early resistance. Some criticism may be anxiety or disguised clarifications. Some issues raised are sure to be bona fide hurdles, and the information will help develop the implementation strategy and priorities. If you can get some of the big obstacles solved early and some of the vocal skeptics on board, then this will create energy for the change and accelerate your business-strategy implementation.

Chapter 9

Establish the Right Drive Team

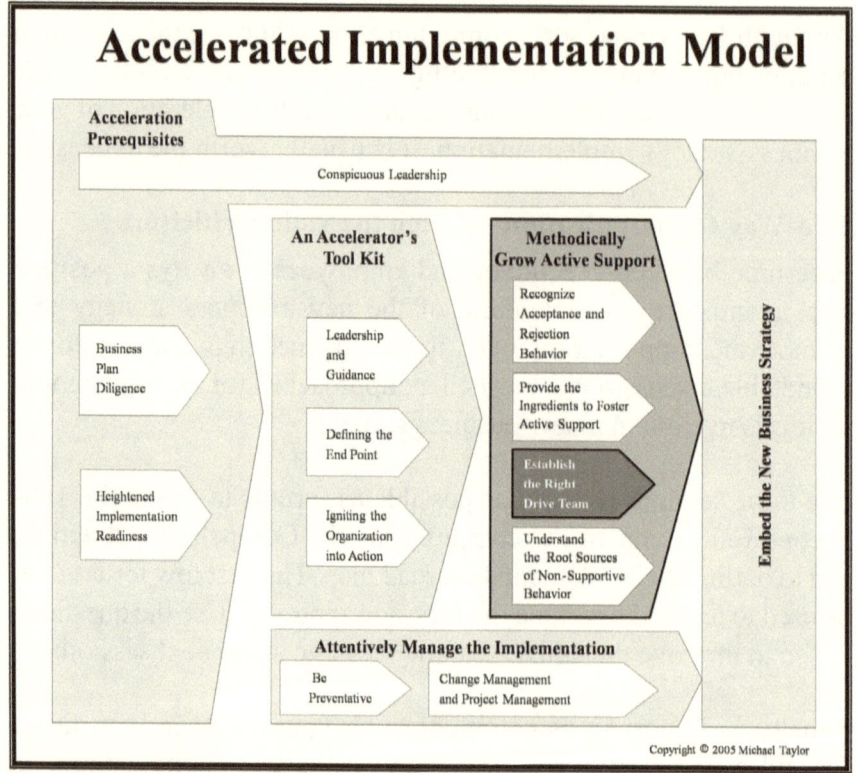

What Is a Drive Team?

The right drive team can enable accelerated adoption of the new business strategy through proactive change management, strong two-way communication, and early resolution of resistance issues.

Even if the people in the organization accept the need for change and accept the new business plan, there will be no real change until someone starts to do something. This usually requires a drive team with important responsibilities:

- to communicate and build support for the new business plan throughout the organization

- to create and execute the implementation or rollout plan

- to recognize and resolve resistance, reluctance, and objections to the new business strategy

Implementing any new business strategy or major initiative is a lot of work. Accelerating the implementation while remaining successful takes a well-orchestrated effort to increase the rate of adoption, drive the speed of the implementation timetable, and increase the impact of implementation activities. This usually takes a team of people in a large organization. Obviously the size of the team and the effort required will be determined by the complexity of the changes required, the amount of variance between the old and the new, the scope of the new strategy, the scope of the affected organization, and the degree of centralization or decentralization of the organization.

This is not a steering committee. This is the implementation-management team, responsible for change management, communications, project management, and delivering the defined implementation outcome on a defined timeline.

Who Should Be Members of the Drive Team?

The drive team should usually consist of two dimensions:

1. Influential members from the management team who can provide leadership and resolve high-level roadblocks, such as an obstructing executive. These prominent people can influence opinion leaders, magnify your message, and give the message credibility.

2. A tactical implementation team to get things done. The tactical change agents provide the "get it done in a way that will work in this organization" expertise.

It is usually a mistake to limit the core drive team to senior executives, because it is too easy to look at macro issues and overlook micro stumbling blocks. This combination of hands-on change agents and influential executive sponsors on the drive team provides an avenue for problems to be identified early, escalated quickly, and resolved rapidly. This accelerates the implementation. This combination also provides a forum to discuss and create detailed rollout plans with a mix of on-the-ground experienced people and the overall organizational perspective of the senior management members.

Make sure you have the right people on your drive team. It is helpful to have executive members who have resources (people and money) that can be applied to the drive team's efforts. In an ideal situation, there is an overlap between the original planning team that did the research and defined the new concept and the implementation drive team. Obviously you don't want saboteurs, but it is also important to avoid lukewarm supporters on your core group. To accelerate the implementation plan, the drive team needs to be a tenacious bunch of go-getters. You will need a core group of people to adhere to the strategy relentlessly. Without strict adherence by the core drive team, the strategy will be manipulated, intentionally misinterpreted, and molded by resistive adopters to reflect the status quo or personal agendas. The stronger the core drive team, the more dedicated they will be and the more effort will be focused on communicating the strategy (the 100-Second Enlightenment and the Compelling Attraction), resolving resistance issues, detailing new processes, etc.

Be cautious of those who instantly become enthusiastic believers of the new strategy. Sometimes these are people who become enthusiastic about anything new and in the long run will not be reliable consistent supporters of the new strategy.

Team building is a good idea. If you can do some team building to gel the core drive team together as one unit, it will make the team a stronger working unit.

Start with a Core Team and Spread

The drive team members are not only the change leaders and implementation managers. The team members are also the opinion influencers and adoption advocates. Often the most effective approaches to encourage adoption of new ideas are parallel efforts that include the communication plan efforts and a methodical process to encourage a rapidly growing number of influential people in the organization to become active supporters and advocates of the new business initiatives. One effective way to accomplish this is to start with a core drive team whose members act as implementation leaders and adoption advocates. Using this core group, you can increase the number of supporters and advocates and spread the acceptance of the new plan through the organization. As mentioned, this is in parallel with all the communication efforts and face-to-face executive presentations in your messaging plan.

It is difficult to create adoption and enthusiasm for the whole population using only a small drive team. The idea here is to start with a small group, the core drive team, and use the drive team to create a growing number of supporters and advocates throughout the organization. At a minimum, you create a large group of people who understand the need for change and understand the new plan. In practice, you can go far beyond that. In practice, you can quickly create a large group of people ready to launch into action and quickly implement the changes from the new initiatives. By doing so, you have paved the way for a smoother rollout of the changes being driven by the new business initiatives.

Methodically you are creating a growing number of enthusiastic supporters who all contribute to the acceptance, adoption, and acceleration of the new business strategy. As the new strategy is unfolded, a growing number of people from each affected group will be added in various capacities to the drive team. The roles of the expanding members of the group will depend on the situation, but their goal is to drive acceptance and adoption of the new way of doing things under the new strategy. In practice, the role of drive team members is to execute the implementation plans, to make sure people understand the new strategy and how it impacts their job and processes, and to solve problems so the new strategy can be implemented as quickly and smoothly as possible. The role of the drive team is to get a growing number of people to actually start doing things the new way under the new strategy.

Structure of the Drive Team

The most effective drive teams are not fragmented; they are a growing team that will eventually include the many people throughout the organization as everyone adopts the new business strategy. Avoiding fragmentation of the team is important to avoid creating islands of information and communication. It is best to keep the team as whole as possible, recognizing the need to break down responsibilities and tasks to subgroups. Sometimes the drive team is organized into a change team and a steering committee, sometimes there are specialty teams, such as a technical design team, and sometimes regional teams or divisional teams are required in widespread or diversified organizations.

For complicated rollouts, you may need various specialty teams—especially if there is a complicated technology change involved. Each specialty team should understand that they are an integral part of the whole drive team and should be included in the overall progress and planning sessions. For complicated situations requiring specialty teams, remember to compose each subteam with a complete roster:

- a senior sponsor who will take an active leadership role on the team

- influential people and opinion leaders

- end users as well as the appropriate specialists (specialists may include technical specialists, communication specialists, data-management specialists, process mappers, focus-group specialists, engineering specialists, marketing specialists, HR specialists, et al.)

- a mix of imaginative, can-do, early adopter, enthusiast types as well as some of the conservative show-me types to make sure that the team has some creative outside-the-box thinking and credibility

Naturally each subgroup or specialty team should have a very clearly defined goal/objective/task and a clear and transparent performance-measurement or milestone expectations communicated.

For large implementation projects with large drive team teams, it is difficult to keep the necessary collegial team spirit strong and keep the team effective without some organization in the team. As you would in any operation, define and communicate responsibilities, performance/progress reporting, organizational structure, authority, decision-making processes, and performance expectations. Communicate with the executives and other stakeholders. It is always a balance to provide sufficient structure to remain an effective functional team as well as remain a flexible creative high-energy group.

A few points need to be mentioned here in the interest of completeness:

- Ensure that the drive team has authority over the resources that are assigned to them.

- Establish reporting and communication lines.

- Establish how often the executive sponsors want progress updates and the substance expectations of the report.

- Establish a process for quick executive decision making when necessary.

Mission-Critical Groups

A new business strategy can have a major impact on a wide number of groups, departments, divisions, or business units. However, there are often a few groups where the major impact will take place. These high-impact groups are usually mission critical to the overall success of the new business plan. In these groups it is important to ensure that every level of management understands and supports the change. Having senior management support in these vital groups is not enough. Very early in the planning process, the management teams from these mission-critical groups should be brought in to ensure that they are all on the same side. It is also important to incorporate their experience in the rollout planning to help avoid problems or delays. Representatives from the mission-critical target groups should be inaugurating members of your core drive team. The drive team representatives from the mission-critical groups should consist of the group's executive leadership, key influence leaders, and those people who will be leading the change efforts.

Executive Empowerment of the Drive Team

The drive team may not have direct authority or control over the target groups affected by the new business strategy, but it should be clear that the drive team has the support of the executive management who does.

The members of the drive team are the change agents with the responsibility to drive, push, and accelerate the adoption of the new business strategy. Change agents get their power to act from a few sources:

- their real authority (which usually is small)

- their influence based on the project being the "right thing to do" for the business

- their implied authority acting on behalf of their executive sponsor

The drive team's implied authority on behalf of the executive team is the most important. This requires the executive leadership to communicate this use of their authority. The question comes up—

which member of the executive leadership team will announce the role and mandate of the drive team? It does not always need to be the CEO. However, if the executive who announces and empowers the drive team does not have real authority over the affected portions of the business, it is likely that the implied authority of change agent will be diminished with these target groups, and it should be expected to have diminished effort or attention applied to requests from the drive team.

Drive Team Success Factors and Common Problems

Ultimately the active supporters of the drive team will spread to include the senior management of all affected divisions or business units, then the middle management, department heads, regional managers, and most importantly frontline managers and supervisors. In the majority of cases, the real acceptance and adoption only really starts when frontline people know that their direct supervisor supports the new strategy and will manage and measure them accordingly.

In reality, in today's business climate we cannot idle the business while we wait to recalibrate our business strategy. We must keep the business operating without a blip and at the same time implement the new business strategy as fast as possible to keep up with competition and a demanding marketplace. This requires extra effort from frontline and middle management in particular. Be on the lookout for a middle or frontline manager who is quietly unsupportive. Their subordinates will interpret their actions as rejection of the new strategy, and the seeds of resistance will grow.

In some cases, an individual manager who is not fully supportive may neutralize the efforts of many others. Their weak support may be the result of a potential loss of power, authority, career opportunity, or other invisible issue. We will discuss these issues in more detail in a later chapter, dealing with sources of resistance. If these weak-supporting managers are highly respected, then a quiet comment by them can send a loud message through the grapevine that "this new strategy is good in theory, but in practice ..." Unfortunately, in the interests of success these dissenting voices may have to be muted by changing these people out of their current position to drive support—especially if they are in a mission-critical group. This is always difficult, because any group, not to mention a mission-critical group, needs a strong leader whom they know and trust in ambiguous times of change. A new manager may not have that relationship with the group.

Normally, portions of an organization will follow the direction of the leader of their group, be it department, region, division, or business unit. The easiest implementation alternative is often the status quo. Sometimes leaders may see the change as a threat and they may drag their feet. These senior and mid-level managers can influence large groups of people. Their influence and their message may be overt, covert, or by osmosis as others see the message coming from the executive team while the manager in question delays or has a lack of action. A key success factor in the efforts to drive acceptance and adoption is to have the leadership of each group become an active supporter and an advocate of the new strategy. The best solution is for key executive leaders to become part of the drive team.

Chapter 10

Understanding the Root Sources
of Non-Supportive Behavior

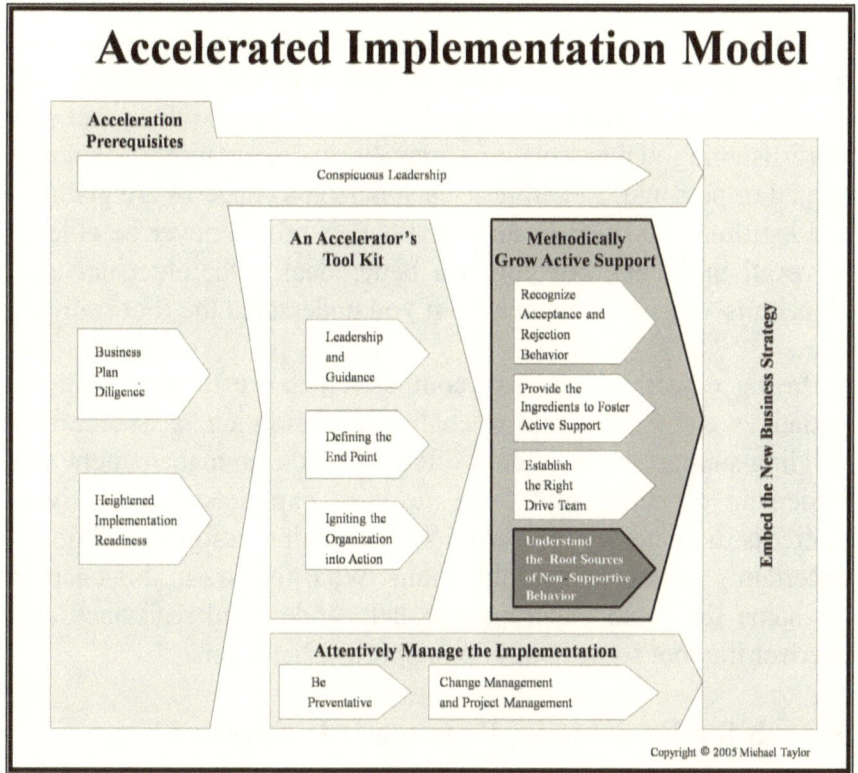

Accelerated Implementation Model

Acceleration Prerequisites

Conspicuous Leadership

An Accelerator's Tool Kit

Methodically Grow Active Support

Business Plan Diligence

Leadership and Guidance

Recognize Acceptance and Rejection Behavior

Provide the Ingredients to Foster Active Support

Defining the End Point

Establish the Right Drive Team

Heightened Implementation Readiness

Igniting the Organization into Action

Understand the Root Sources of Non-Supportive Behavior

Embed the New Business Strategy

Attentively Manage the Implementation

Be Preventative

Change Management and Project Management

Copyright © 2005 Michael Taylor

The Root Source of Non-Supportive Behavior Is an Individual Matter

"Resistance" and "resistive behavior" are general terms that usually refer to any evidence of reluctance, objections, or non-supportive behavior. Resistance is often referred to as a group response. For example, the logistics group always resists any process changes, or the sales organization always resists any change to their negotiation reports. Resistance does not start as a group behavior. Reluctance, objections, and non-supporting behavior starts as individual matters. Although there may be some initial group behavior, supporting a new idea is an individual decision. The best advice is to listen very carefully and try to find the underlying individual reasons for objections and reluctance.

Recognize that each person sincerely believes that his or her point of view is legitimate. Really listen to them completely. Repeat their concerns back to them. This not only ensures that you understand what they were trying to say but also demonstrates to them that you were listening. Their concerns may be major or minor, business related or personal. Regardless, each person's concerns are genuine and legitimate to them as an individual. You will never be able to solve all problems, but you can better deal with reluctance and objections—resistive behavior—if you understand the root sources.

Diffusing objections and overcoming reluctance to new business initiatives can be a complex challenge. Resolving resistance and building support for new ideas often stretches the management and leadership capabilities of even the most experienced executives. There is no surefire prescription that helps resolve individual uncertainty or unexpected objections. What follows in this chapter are some tips from experience to help understand resistance and uncover the root sources of non-supportive behavior.

Search for Resistance, Because It Is Surely There

We can describe resistance to the new business strategy as anxiety, reluctance, objection, or outright obstruction and sabotage. Some resistance is easier to recognize than others. It may be overt or covert.

The overt resistance is easy to see, and it may actually be constructive by pointing out obstacles to your success. On the other hand, overt resistance can be a delaying or avoidance tactic. Sometimes it is a mid-level manager proving his or her authority, independence, or organizational influence by demonstrating that he or she run their own business and they do not have to follow head office edicts. Some overt resistance may simply be the disbelief that the new strategy is "the right thing to do" for the business or a temporary distraction—simply another "program of the month" that will go away. The good news is that for this type of resistance it is often easier to identify the author of the contravening message and you can address their issues and try to resolve them. Covert resistance provides greater challenges.

Sometimes there are highly vocal people who will openly tell you that they disagree with the new business strategy, but more frequently the resistance is "underground." Covert resistance is a symptom, for which it is often difficult to find the cause. Even if you can find the author of a pocket of resistance—the person who is sowing the seeds of objections—it may be difficult to get to the real root issue that is driving their opinion and behavior. When asked why they object to the need for change or to the new business strategy, they offer facts supporting their view. Occasionally there are individuals who will always find a critical obstacle that, when solved, is followed by yet another claimed-to-be-critical obstacle that will require more research, thinking, or analysis. The true challenge here is not to exhaust the objective arguments but to try to uncover the underlying, often personal and sensitive, issue that is driving the author's opinion. It may be job security, the breakup of a workgroup of colleagues, or another personal issue. More on personal issues later. As we said, resistance is a symptom and is something you need to tune into in order to recognize it. Below is a list of some typical symptoms that may indicate there is an underlying issue that needs to be uncovered and resolved.

Some typical symptoms:

- lack of resources by managers, or they provide low-level resources who cannot make commitments

- last-minute notices that people cannot attend critical planning or implementation meetings

- the CEO or senior executive is needed to persuade someone to come to a planning meeting

- missed deadlines and/or no commitment to deadlines

- passive agreement, not real agreement

- disinterest in meetings

- reduction or stoppage in participation in meetings

- the message that a manager has given to their department is different from the vision you are working toward

- no commitment to change the measurement method or the compensation plan

- growth in counterproductive gossip and rumors

- sudden or unexplained decrease in quality or productivity

- increase in absenteeism

- sabotage

- resignation—employees leaving

- closed body language

- increased grievances

I started out by saying, "Search for the resistance, because it is surely there." I accept that the amount of resistance varies directly with the speed of implementation and how extreme the required change is. However, the amount of resistance may also be your barometer of the effectiveness of the communication plan, the implementation plan, your change methods, or the new business strategy. The key is listening and uncovering the root issues behind the resistance. A ramrod implementation approach will almost always evoke the most resistance and offers the highest risk of failure. On the other hand, the missionary approach will almost always result in the longest implementation period and offers the highest risk of accomplishing nothing. Finding the balance requires attentive management.

Investigate Resistive Behavior: There Is a Reason for It

Resistance displays itself in behaviors. Rather than recognizing resistive behaviors, we often categorize the people demonstrating the non-supporting behavior as "not bought in" or "dissenters" or "obstacles" or "problems." It is not uncommon to go one step further and start to consider them in groups: "the XYZ department is putting up barriers." These are dangerous conclusions. First, as was mentioned earlier, resistive behavior or non-supporting behavior is a symptom of an underlying reason or root issue. Second, we must never lose sight of the fact that although a group may be supportive, ambivalent, reluctant, or resistive, the underlying reasons driving that behavior will be individual personal reasons that differ from person to person. It is not unrealistic for a strong group leader to influence the opinion of the whole group just because the followers do not want to step out of line with their boss.

From my experience, the most common reasons why people demonstrate non-supportive behavior to new business ideas fall into several categories:

- They have a legitimate concern or see a legitimate flaw in the plan, a flaw that needs to be fixed.

- They have a lack of information, they have inaccurate information, or they doubt the credibility of the information that has been presented to them.

- The change resulting from the new business plan has a negative impact on them personally.

- The changes require them to work outside their comfort zone temporarily or permanently. This may be a skill or experience comfort zone or a psychological or emotional comfort zone (e.g., loss of control).

- The change requires them to work outside their peak expertise zone. In other words, they will not be able to be as proficient or successful. This can have an impact on their self-esteem, status, compensation, or career.

- It just doesn't feel right.

Resistive behavior results from normal human reactions; it is not abnormal or out of the ordinary. The key is to uncover the root cause of the behavior. You may have to do some real digging and spend time with the affected people to develop their trust to a point where they will confide the underlying truth to you. It may be difficult for them to discuss some issues, such as their own vulnerabilities.

Once you understand some of the root reasons for the non-supporting behavior, you can begin to address them. There will almost always be a combination of things and not just one issue. Nevertheless, people will sometimes vocalize the one issue that they feel is the most credible, and it is rarely the psychological or emotional fears such as loss of control. More on psychological and emotional issues later. The lesson we draw from this is that resistive behavior is a symptom of an underlying reason. We must discover and address the reason and not be fooled into reacting to the symptom.

Listen for Legitimate Concerns or Flaws in the Business Plan

If, in your view, the organization largely accepts the need for change and understands the benefits but individuals are not demonstrating support for the new business strategy, perhaps this is because they see some inherent flaws. Your frontline people may understand some tactical aspects that are not obvious to senior management and that have not been considered.

The flaws may or may not be legitimate. However, your front-line people may be uncomfortable pointing this out.

In most cases people will be supportive if they see the change as positive. If they believe that the new model is flawed, then they will not support it and you will have great difficulty getting them on board and gaining even passive support for the new strategy. It is critical to have strong leadership in times of change, but it is equally important not to have blind and stubborn leadership. Listen carefully to frontline feedback; it may actually accelerate implementation.

A few years ago I was involved in implementing a new sales tool that was intended to help the salespeople capture important selling features and competitive information that would help improve their chances of success of a given sales contract. Soon we received some feedback indicating that the idea was not worth the effort and should be scrapped. We were convinced that the initiative was a good idea and were keen to implement it. Upon further investigation, we found that in certain portions of the business the sales reps were right. We altered our plans and only proceeded with implementation in the groups where there was value in doing so.

Check to See if the Message Has Been Received and Understood

Too often communication is a one-way transmit and no effort is made to confirm if the message was received: "I sent an e-mail." "I did a presentation." "It was in the newsletter."

There are two aspects to remember to confirm that your communications efforts have been successful; first, message received; and second, message understood. You have to confirm both.

First, communicating the message. All experienced communicators and adult educators know that adults effectively receive information in various styles. Some internalize information best when it is explained to them, others do better with diagrams, and others do better with a document they can read and review. Often the same explanation needs to be explained in various ways for everyone to understand. Some understand complicated topics better with analogies, while others need to have the new strategy explained in the context of their specific job function.

Second, understanding the message. Each person will have their individual and natural process of learning and understanding the new business strategy or the new business model. Don't mistake their questions as non-supportive or resistive behavior.

As often as possible it is important to deliver mission-critical messages, such as a new business strategy, face-to-face to as many employees as possible. Give time for questions. Often people are reluctant to ask a question in a large forum, so make alternative avenues available, anonymous and not. Meet with small groups and ask frontline supervisors to forward any lingering questions later.

Most business changes do not affect everyone to the same extent. There will be some individuals who will experience a major impact personally, while others may see a minor impact. The impact could be to their responsibilities, work environment, or many other aspects. For those people who are about to experience a major change as a result of the new business initiatives, you can expect them to have questions with a large component of personal and psychological matters, and they are more likely to want to speak in small groups or individually to their local supervisor.

Occasionally the message of the new business strategy is complete but not believed. It is received by people in the organization, who wonder if this new strategy is simply a "program of the month." Their reaction is usually to wait and see if the new strategy stays or is replaced by the next "program of the month." This is particularly true if the organization has a history of failed changes or superficial attempts at projects. This reaction can have a dramatic impact on the acceleration of your new business strategy and must be addressed quickly. Often a review of the market forces that are driving the need for change, an explanation of the diligence in the development of the strategy, and a commitment of resources to implement the new plan will help get over this hurdle.

The CEO cannot visit every employee. Somehow you need to get a fully articulated message to everyone affected by the new business strategy if they are going to be able to support it. The Compelling Attraction discussed earlier is a powerful enabling tool to help middle managers and frontline managers accomplish this. The detailed description in the Compelling Attraction will answer many of the common concerns like the following:

- What will my job be?

- Who will my boss be?

- Will I like my new work environment?

- Will I like my work?

- Will my compensation be impacted?

- Will I have a job or will I be laid off?

Listen for Concerns Based on Lack of Information or Inaccurate Information

One of the most common problems, especially in large or decentralized organizations, is getting an accurate and complete understanding of the message. It is hard to understand the reasons driving the need for change or understand the new business strategy if you have incomplete or inaccurate information—especially if you are not aware that the information is incomplete or inaccurate. It is easy for someone with inaccurate information to conclude that the business strategy is flawed or that senior management is incompetent based on the facts in front of them. Inaccurate or incomplete information can quickly extinguish support and stall your accelerated implementation.

The only way to test message accuracy and completeness is for senior management to sample the organization by spending time in discussion and listening, face-to-face, to people in frontline parts of the organization. If you rely on feedback from frontline managers, they too may have incomplete information.

Listen for Concerns about the Negative Impact the Change Will Have on Individuals

The most powerful force in the organization is the behavior driven by "what's in it for me." A new business strategy impacts the roles, responsibilities, and careers of individual people. The negative impact that individuals expect to experience as a result of the new plan can create an insurmountable barrier to implementation if not disarmed or resolved.

Sometimes the perceived negative impact is simply a misunderstanding of the impact of the new strategy and can be resolved with discussion and accurate information. Sometimes a negative impact on individuals is unavoidable, and counterproductive behavior is not unexpected. The best thing to do is to empathetically assist those individuals through the difficult times.

I have witnessed a number of common concerns across a variety of situations:

- Job functions that are negatively impacted: responsibility, tasks, activities, flexibility, work patterns, work environment, or location.

- Work culture that is negatively impacted: loss of colleagues or the micro-culture of a working group.

- Change in responsibility that is outside an individual's preference zone (what they enjoy doing), or capability zone (what they have the ability to be successful at).

- Loss of momentum: "I was so in tune with my job, and the knowledge required that I could be successful easily. I was on track for a progression in my career."

- Longer-term concerns: "How will my value to the company change?" "Will I be able to be successful?" "Will my intellectual property (knowledge and experience) be as valuable?" "How will my performance be measured (fear of incompetence)?" "Will I be perceived poorly because I am unfamiliar in this environment—by management or by my peers?"

- The impact on compensation, especially in roles that have a significant variable portion of compensation.

- The impact of failure: "The new business approach sounds good, but it might fail, and failure would be worse that the status quo. Even though I believe in the merit of making the change, I am better off the way things are now than I would be if it fails. The failure could be during the implementation or that the actual new business model is flawed."

- Non-job-related disruption: The changes resulting from the new business strategy may affect job requirements and consequently may affect other things that are invisible to management; for example, commute time, picking up a child at day care, soccer practice, volunteer work, social activities, etc.

The Hierarchy of Employment Needs; Psychological and Emotional Ties

I am not a psychologist and have not studied psychology, but I have witnessed a lot of behavior that has been sparked by a changing work environment and is driven by psychological and emotional needs. I do think that there is a hierarchy of employment needs. The first and most essential need is for secure employment and the associated secure income to provide for the necessities of life. The next level of employment need is success; that is, being in a job that fits your skills and allows you to conduct that job with some level of proficiency and potential for advancement to fit your skills. The third level is enjoyment: being in a job you enjoy doing in a work environment that you enjoy being part of.

Hierarchy of Employment Needs

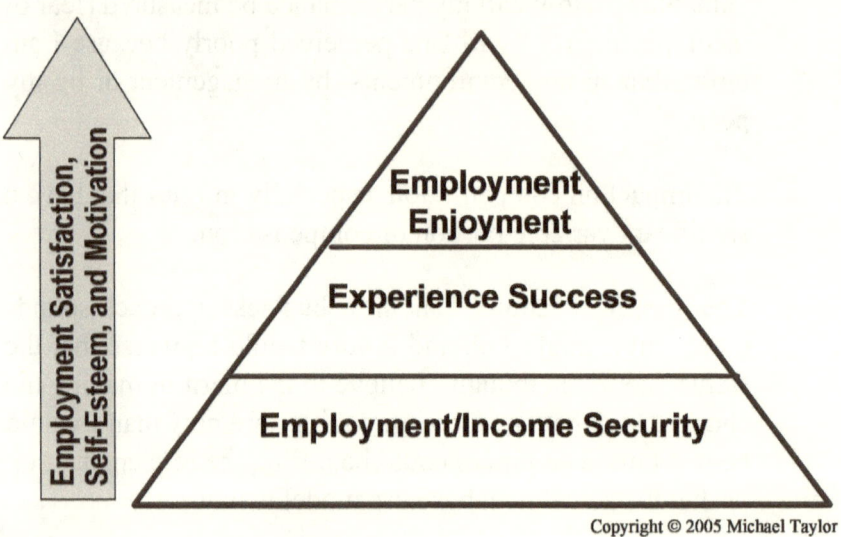

The outcome of the employment hierarchy is job satisfaction, self-esteem, and motivation. At the highest level we observe high self-esteem, a sense of belonging, a high level of pride, people who identify their work life as part of who they are as a person, microcultures of work groups who socialize outside of work, and a general level of trust rather than suspicion in management and the organization.

Your existing work environment may not be like the idealistic description above, but such environments do exist and I hope you have the opportunity to experience them. Nevertheless, in most established functioning organizations some level of job satisfaction exists for the majority of people, with pockets of the organization that are operating very high on the employment hierarchy. A new business strategy may be an essential change for the success of the company. It may be the best strategy in the current situation. However, the new strategy can result in changes to job functions and work environments that disturb the underlying factors that are providing the existing job satisfaction. Don't underestimate the amount of reluctance or non-supportive behavior or outright counterproductive or even destructive behavior that may result.

These are difficult issues to discover. The underlying rationale is often very personal and involves topics that individuals do not want to talk about, especially with someone from outside their group. It often involves a change in a work group, a loss of control, a disruption of routine, habits, and orderliness, a concern about being able to be hold the same level of proficiency with the same effort, or a concern about working outside their preference zone or capability zone: "I have lost something I have been a part of, am proud of, and have some loyalty to."

What can help? There is no single answer. There will be no single fix. Perhaps getting these affected people involved with the implementation planning so they start to get a feeling for it, take out some of the uncertainty, and allow them to feel like the outcome somehow partially belongs to them could be helpful. In some cases, for some people there will be a strong sense of loss. Our overall business objective is to accelerate the implementation of the new business strategy while recognizing that we need our experienced talent to be supportive and motivated. To minimize the counterproductive behavior and work through some of the transition concerns, it is important that we recognize these emotional ties so we can, in the end, create new high-satisfaction work environments.

The experts tell us that there are five emotional stages of loss (the Kuble-Ross model - 1969): denial, anger, bargaining, depression, and acceptance. They tell us to let the people involved work through it and support the people through it. Like I said at the beginning, I am not a psychologist, but maybe in some situations the five stages of loss apply to the loss of camaraderie and routine that results in a major business change. The best thing we can do is to help our people through it.

A Few Points, from Experience, to Help Understand Resistive Behavior

You Cannot Overcommunicate

To accelerate the business strategy, you will need as many people as possible actively supporting the implementation. This can only be done if they know and understand what they are working toward. It will be hard for them to be motivated if they don't understand why the new business strategy is implemented.

One of the most important keys to accelerating the business-strategy implementation is Communication, Communication, Communication.

Initial Caution Is Natural

It is natural for people to react cautiously to the launch announcement of a major change. People normally experience some level of anxiety about a disturbance to their routine or an uncertain future. It is common for people to be reluctant about change rather than enthusiastic. Your task is to calm the initial cautionary feelings that create anxiety and set the stage for rational consideration of the proposed new ideas. The 100-Second Enlightenment and the Compelling Attraction will prove to be useful tools to help diffuse some of this initial anxiety and create interest in the new initiatives. Every ounce of resistance that is avoided or resolved quickly is worth 100 pounds of support for an accelerated implementation.

Get It Right the First Time

It is faster and easier to explain the new business initiatives the first time than it is to try to re-explain the portions of the message that were incorrect or incomplete. Correcting an incorrect or incomplete message creates new problems of credibility in the leadership team and suspicion that you are making this up as you go along. It is important to make sure all communication—including the 100-

Second Enlightenment and the Compelling Attraction—is well vetted and air tight.

Look for Transition Burnout

The pace of the world is accelerating. Competitive intensity is increasing in an unprecedented fashion. Change is constant. Now let's bring this down to the local business situation. Just to stay abreast of the market and ahead of competition, many organizations find themselves with few times of stability. The mantra is "constant change." What does this mean to the business leader who is trying to accelerate the implementation of a new business strategy? We frequently turn to a core group of people to lead a variety of initiatives. Few people can run on the edge all the time. Everyone needs time to stabilize. Stress is cumulative. Not only project leaders but target groups within the organization who have endured a large change need time to stabilize before embarking on another large transition. They may resist or simply emotionally opt out to provide a period of emotional stability and intellectual rest. This may not be possible in a crisis. If they are burned out, then add new people and re-calibrate your expectations accordingly.

Some People Think a Miracle Happens and the Change Is Done

It always amazes me that some people think a miracle happens immediately following the initial launch announcement and the new strategy is implemented overnight. Then frustration sets in and support diminishes because their expectations were not met.

It surprises me how many people have some idea that we announce a new business strategy or a major change and somehow overnight they will start seeing the differences. It is usually naiveté that drives these perceptions. However, some people expect that the infrastructure is in place immediately. This causes frustration and skepticism when this support is not there on day one. Some employees view these systems as mission critical from their perspective and start to wonder about the management's competence and the plan's credibility if the systems are not there on day one. Many people in the front line of the organization do not have any experience with infrastructure systems or major business changes and naturally do not realize the importance of these systems or the effort and time required to make the transition in these systems. They often are not familiar with the intricacies of the systems and believe it is a matter of a small "overnight" reconfiguration. The reason I am pointing this out is to suggest that you include some information in your launch announcement about the infrastructure changes required and the approximate time frame expected for these changes to take place.

On a positive note, once it is explained, the vast majority of people quickly appreciate the complexities of infrastructure systems, the importance of controlled change management, and the value of documenting all changes and going through the effort of updating policies, processes, and procedures.

Handle Objections as Genuine Serious Concerns

These are real people with real concerns—take their objections seriously. What may be a small or insignificant issue to you may be a major issue to the person voicing the concern. Resist the urge to view criticism as resistance. Look at the situation as resolving the tactical issues of the new business strategy. The people voicing concerns are actually helping you. Acknowledge the issue directly to the person voicing the concern. Remember that the people you are dealing with are often frustrated. Balance the need to be aggressive, to accelerate the implementation, with empathy. Some people will be bringing issues forward in an attempt to help. Others will be voicing opinions because they disagree with some of the ideas or conclusions in the business approach. Remember that people do not change their position on an idea in an instant. Take the time to discuss it and understand their point of view and explain yours. In the end you will need a growing number of supporters, not saboteurs.

Get a Sense of the Intensity and Magnitude of Critical Resistance Issues

Get a sense of the strength of the resistance—each individual or group or each issue. Sometimes it is useful to categorize the magnitude or intensity or criticality of an issue. This will allow you to prioritize where you will focus energy. Some critical issues may require a lot of attention and "handholding." Some less-critical issues may be addressed with newsletters or all employee presentations or town hall meetings.

Part IV

Attentively Manage the Implementation

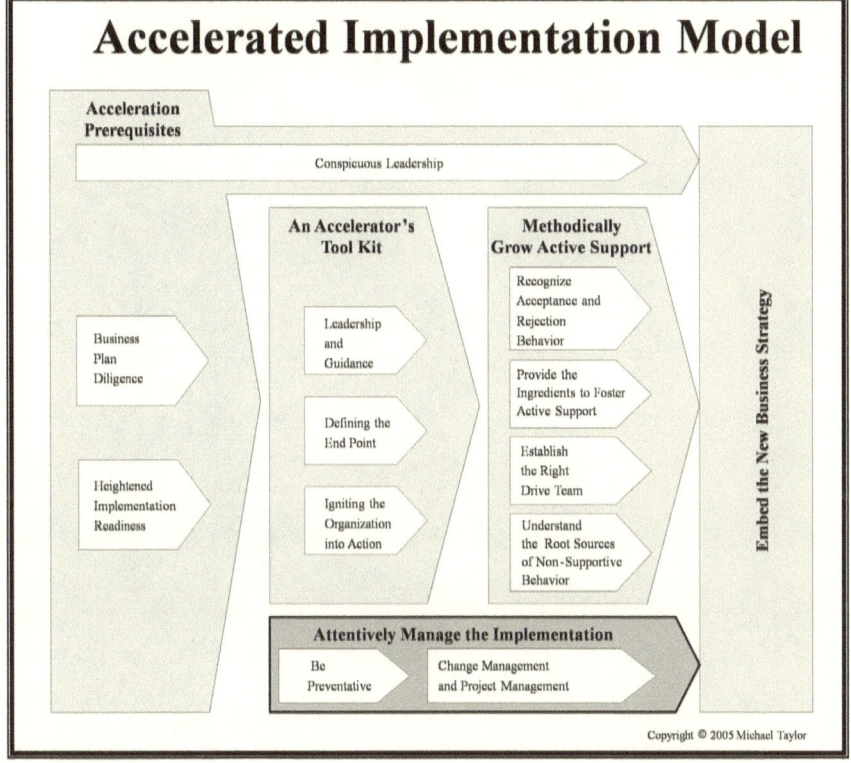

Introduction

We have spent much of this book so far discussing preparation and preventative measures that can make the implementation of major business initiatives go more smoothly and can successfully accelerate them. Even though these are all important ingredients, this is not all. Attentively managing the implementation of your new strategy is equally critical to accelerated success.

This book is not a detailed look at project management. Much has been written about that subject elsewhere. This book focuses on practical approaches, provides tips to help make business-strategy implementation more effective, and outlines common pitfalls that can unnecessarily delay success. This section focuses on two areas: First, a series of tips that will help you avoid common problems and delays that slow the adoption of the new business strategy. Second, a few points from experience about change management and project management that can help you avoid unnecessary delays while making the implementation go smoother.

The points outlined in this section are not from any theory or ideology. These tips are from experience.

Chapter 11

Be Preventative—Tips from Experience

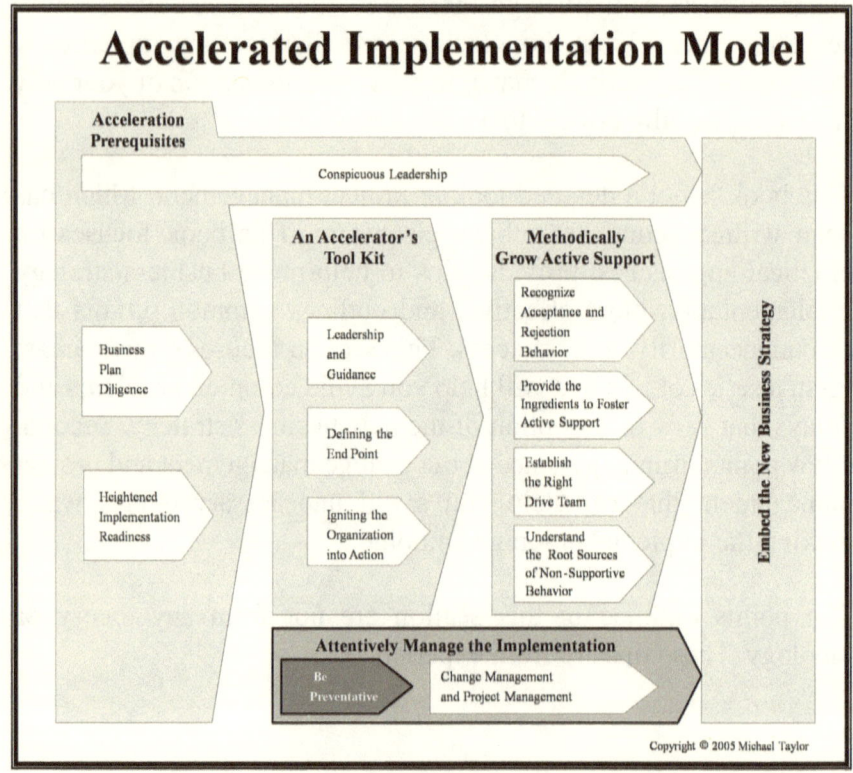

Accelerated Implementation Model

Acceleration Prerequisites

Conspicuous Leadership

An Accelerator's Tool Kit

Methodically Grow Active Support

Business Plan Diligence

Leadership and Guidance

Recognize Acceptance and Rejection Behavior

Defining the End Point

Provide the Ingredients to Foster Active Support

Heightened Implementation Readiness

Igniting the Organization into Action

Establish the Right Drive Team

Understand the Root Sources of Non-Supportive Behavior

Embed the New Business Strategy

Attentively Manage the Implementation

Be Preventative

Change Management and Project Management

Copyright © 2005 Michael Taylor

Demonstrate Top-to-Bottom Management Support

Deliver a Consistent Message from Top to Bottom

The speed of adoption for any new initiative is influenced by a number of factors, including the message from the management team. If people in the organization sense that the management team is not fully supportive of the new strategy, reluctance in the organization will grow and the enthusiasm for implementation will be difficult to generate. It is generally perceived that the leadership team has better insight into the strategy than the rank and file does. Consequently, if the leadership is not supportive, there must be a reason. This goes beyond the senior team. Frontline people in the organization, where real implementation and support occurs, often are informed about major changes during employee meetings, by e-mail, or by a notice. These frontline employees often look to their first-line supervisor to confirm or clarify the news.

As an implementation leader, there is an opportunity to begin to set the stage for accelerated adoption if the message from the two sources, executive and frontline supervisor, is consistent and positive. The inference of the consistent message is that the whole chain in between is on board. A strong consistent message delivered throughout the management hierarchy is perceived as an indicator of consensus support of the whole organization of the new strategy, resulting in an initial boost of confidence in the new strategy. This helps set the stage for welcome adoption and accelerated implementation.

Consistency in Behavior and Message

Confidence in the new business initiative is a thin veneer at first and will be tested frequently. It is common for managers to be peppered with the same question from various people asked in different ways to test for consistency in the answer. In addition, the words and actions of executives will be observed closely to check for inconsistency between their behavior and their message. Management behavior and especially the decisions they make will receive heightened scrutiny by people in the organization to confirm consistency or to look for anything that may question the management support or credibility of the new strategy. The old adage holds true:

> *Walk the walk;*
> *talk the talk;*
> *behavior, behavior, behavior;*
> *every manager—all the time.*

Use Key Phrases to Strengthen Consistency

Business strategies are often complex. To help build a consistent message, it helps to identify a few core messages. It is often helpful and necessary to explain the elements of the new business strategy in different ways to help people understand the message. However, never lose sight of the importance of a consistent message. The organization will be looking for it. The core message can provide this consistency, even to the point of using the same key words or phrases to build a consistent message and begin to develop the vocabulary of the new strategy.

Maximize Face Time

In the early stages of communicating the new strategy, plan for as much face-to-face time as possible by senior executives, with as much of the organization as possible. It is much easier to develop confidence in an idea—the new business strategy—if the leadership team can develop confidence in their ability to be successful.

Continuously Build Trust, Confidence, and Credibility, Over and Over

Trust, confidence, and credibility are never absolute or permanent. The adoption of your new business strategy will be faster if the organization has a high degree of trust and confidence in the management team. In times of change, trust, confidence, and the credibility of the management team can all be brought into question. In times of change, such as the implementation of a new business strategy, people in the organization often experience changes in their work environment, job routines, and social cultures at work. This often causes anxiety and weakens the organization's confidence in the management team. New messages from management will cause increased scrutiny, discussion, and questions. Without trust, confidence, and credibility, the required implementation effort will be much greater and the progress will be much slower.

It is important to add ingredients to your implementation plan that will foster adoption rather than resistance to the new initiatives. The credibility of the business strategy and leadership team will be questioned many times over as people in the organization seek reassurance that the organization is on the path to success.

The leadership team's credibility is built on a foundation of trust. Trust is something that takes time to develop, but it can evaporate instantaneously for the smallest reason. The old saying "one bad apple spoils the barrel" applies here. In every group of people there will be some who are naturally suspicious of the leadership team and will be on the lookout for hidden agendas or concealed motives. People are anxious in times of change and will look for the slightest evidence of misinformation from the leadership team or look for senior management actions that are inconsistent with the stated strategy. This can call into question the trust of the entire leadership team, the credibility of the new business strategy, and everything that has been communicated about it. A lack of trust can develop a lack of cooperation and covert unstated reasons for reluctance to participate in your implementation plans. Mistrust is one of the hardest types of resistance to overcome.

The importance of the communication plan in any new initiative is common knowledge. In addition to your message, the leadership team must continuously reinforce their credibility and demonstrate the credibility of the business strategy to reduce anxiety in the organization and build confidence in the success of the new plan.

Executives sometimes fall into the trap of focusing on the strategy message and bypassing an explanation of the diligence that went into the strategy development and a description of the experience the leadership team brings to this challenge. It is important that a critical mass of the organization has confidence that this is the right business strategy, the right implementation plan, the right leadership team, and the right implementation drive team to be successful.

As the new business strategy is executed, people in the organization will be reminded of the implementation difficulties over and over as they face the associated daily challenges. It is important to frequently remind them of the benefits of the new strategy. It is also important to continuously strengthen trust, confidence, and credibility in the new strategy and the leadership team.

Establish Urgency, Communicate Incessantly, and Create an Army of Communicators at Least Three Times Over

The obvious enemies of accelerated implementation are those people who are strong resistors and vocal objectors. Equally as dangerous are those people who are doing nothing to support you, who steadfastly stick to existing methods, or who believe that the new strategy is the latest "program of the month" that will soon pass. To accelerate your business-strategy implementation, you need to develop a sense of urgency in the organization and a critical mass of active supporters. This requires a lot of communication effort. The more radical the new business strategy compared is to the existing situation, the more important this is.

Skeptics and resisters will be the first to fall back into the old ways. Remember that you are paddling upstream, and the first lull in effort will spur some people to drift back to the old methods and encourage others to join them. Communicate incessantly.

A small group of management and communication people cannot be the only voice of explanation or support for the new business plan. In addition to using traditional communication tools such as employee meetings, e-mail, Web meetings, and newsletters, you must create an army of communicators. Proactive communication and enthusiasm is contagious and often difficult to accomplish. Layer upon layer of management, department upon department, division after division, business unit after business unit, region after region, must hear the message, understand the reason for the change, accept the new business strategy, and grow to actively support an accelerated implementation. This is a lot of work, but this is part of the investment required for accelerated implementation.

Experience has shown us that just when you yourself are getting tired of repeating the message over and over and you think everyone in the organization must be fully informed, there is someone somewhere in the organization who is just hearing it for the first time. This is especially true in widely decentralized organizations.

Often it is helpful to explain the message in different ways because we know that individuals learn and absorb new information in various ways. It is helpful to explain the logic and rationale for the new business strategy. It may also be helpful to include examples and analogies. Include diagrams, charts, and explanatory graphics in your materials, because many people are visual learners. Always provide written explanations of your message because some individuals need to take the time to quietly read and reread the information to absorb it. Give everyone access to as much information as possible. We sometimes mistakenly underestimate the level of interest and understanding that people in our organizations have about our market, our company, and our success. Communicate effectively without information overload, but make as much information as possible available. All of this is a lot of work, but this is the investment required for accelerated implementation.

If that is not enough, there's more. Experience has shown us that each person needs to hear the message three times over—that is, they need to hear it at three different sessions. Successful leaders sometimes introduce more granularity each time. Use the follow-up session to confirm and re-confirm that the decisions made are proving to be the right ones. Communicate the progress and communicate any early success. Communicate the difficulties your competitors are having who did not follow your path. Competitor difficulties are a proxy for what you would have looked like if you did not adopt the new strategy.

This is a lot of work, but this is the investment required for accelerated implementation.

Publicize Early Successes; Boost Adoption

Nothing boosts confidence like success. When you start to experience success, publish it to the organization as fast as possible. Success does not have to be financial growth. Success can be progress—the completion of implementation phases, overcoming hurdles, or the growth of the number of individuals adopting a new work process. Communicate the heck out of them. Don't save up for a large communication. Communicating frequently about small successes can be very effective. Communicating early successes fuels the adoption of the new strategy. People have lingering reluctance for a long time. A stream of successes says, "See, it was the right thing to do."

Communication of early successes should recognize the efforts by everyone contributing and include the difficulty faced by those impacted. This demonstrates that our strategy may be challenging but confirms that we are on the right path.

Celebrate early successes and recognize the effort that everyone has put into the whole project. At the early stages when successes are still few it is important to recognize the effort that everyone is contributing. Acknowledge the people who demonstrate the new desired behavior. Celebrations can be employee meetings, newsletters, company events, or prizes. Celebrations should be as public as appropriately possible in the organization to recognize and promote adoption of the new strategy. (*Caution*: Don't let a celebration indicate completion. The last thing you want to do is to prematurely evaporate the sense of urgency and the energy required for the implementation efforts.)

Finally, early success should be rewarded. To accelerate business-strategy implementation it may be appropriate to be creative and flexible with your performance-measurement system. The early stages of implementation are critical to drive the behavior and adoption your want. The performance or incentive system is a way that management can demonstrate they are "putting their money where their mouth is."

Ready Is the First Part of Ready-Set-Go

Be proactive: Improve the organization's change readiness. Inform people about the dynamics of change and change management without self-inducing anxiety or alarm.

As you introduce your new business strategy to the organization, it is helpful to introduce everyone to the expected dynamics of change and change management. Many of the people affected by the new business plan will appreciate and cooperate more if they understand the dynamics of change management. This will allow them to see that what may look like chaos is an organized process of change. They will better accept the lack of order for a period of time if they understand the normal expectations, dynamics, and feelings during a major change.

The more aware the organization is about implementation processes and normal dynamics in these circumstances, the less apprehension they are likely to experience and consequently, the more likely they will look at new things with an evaluative eye rather than putting up the wall of opposition to something new. Consider this resistance prevention medicine. You are preparing the organization to support the new business strategy and to support the implementation team rather than the organization's gravitating toward objections, reluctance, and resistance. What you are doing is increasing the nimbleness of the organization and making them ready for a dynamic period. Of course this does not diminish the need for strong leadership and a strong implementation drive team to accelerate the business-strategy implementation.

As we all know the only constant is change. The trend is accelerated change. To remain successful, organizations will need to become more agile. Readiness to accept change is a core attitude requirement. Change management is a core aptitude (skill and readiness) requirement.

Take the Acid Test for Implementation Readiness

It is easy to get caught up in the urgency of the new business strategy and prematurely jump to implementation before you and the organization are ready. Take the time to review this quick checklist. Experience has shown us that these elements are critical prerequisites that, if missing, will cause unnecessary resistance, slower adoption, duplicated efforts, and increased implementation expense, and most important, will cause delays.

- diligent review of the critical bits of the business justification

- senior management team commitment to the new strategy

- a documented Compelling Attraction

- an acceptance of the need to change by a critical mass of management ranks

- an acceptance of the new business strategy and implementation strategy by a critical mass of the management ranks

- a commitment by the management team to invest in the necessary resources and communication effort

- mission-critical groups that have been identified with plans in place to build early adoption in these groups

- a communication plan that

    - outlines the need for change, the Compelling Attraction, and a sense of urgency

    - strengthens confidence in the "rightness" of the new plan and confidence in the management team and the organization's ability to be successful with the new plan

Chapter 12

Change Management and Project Management
Tips from Experience

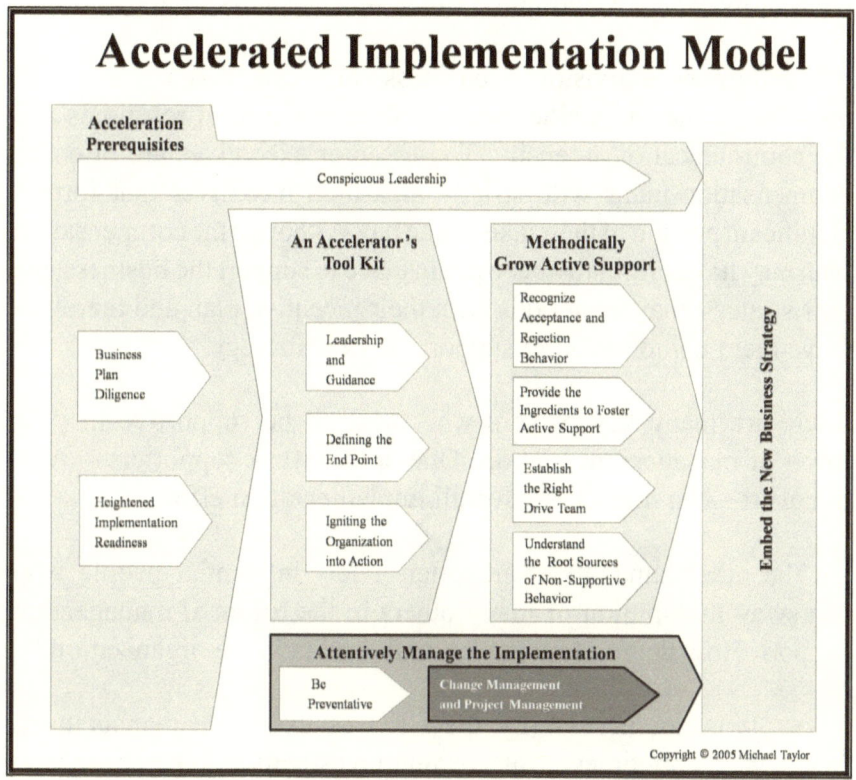

Accelerated Implementation Model

Acceleration Prerequisites

Conspicuous Leadership

An Accelerator's Tool Kit

Methodically Grow Active Support

Business Plan Diligence

Leadership and Guidance

Recognize Acceptance and Rejection Behavior

Provide the Ingredients to Foster Active Support

Defining the End Point

Establish the Right Drive Team

Heightened Implementation Readiness

Igniting the Organization into Action

Understand the Root Sources of Non-Supportive Behavior

Embed the New Business Strategy

Attentively Manage the Implementation

Be Preventative

Change Management and Project Management

Copyright © 2005 Michael Taylor

As mentioned in the introduction to this section, this book is not a detailed account of project management or change management. However, project management and change management are both critical elements. What follows in this chapter is not a "how to" guide but rather an account of tips from experience on these two topics. These tips will help accelerate the implementation of your new business strategy.

Build and Validate a Leadership Tower of Support

Build a leadership tower—support from the foundation (frontline management) to the CEO. This may seem obvious, but any experienced manager knows that the organization does not always follow the CEO's instructions with the same vigor. Without broad leadership support in the mission-critical groups in the organization, there are sure to be delays, a lack of resources, inadequate communication, and a slow expensive adoption of the new business strategy.

At a minimum, a division or business unit's executive management must be on the same side, because they can control resources and the communication intensity. These senior executives are often on compensation plans with strictly measured incentives that form a significant portion of their take-home pay. Although the compensation plan may have originally been put in place to support the business, the new strategy may be at odds with their incentive plan and therefore leave them unmotivated to support the new strategy.

There are many key players who must all be supportive in your tower of management support. One or two weak supporters—overt or covert—can impact the overall implementation effort.

On the other hand, there are often a few influential people who can sway the opinion of many others in the tower of management support. How do you find the key influencers in the organization?

- It is not necessarily the CEO or executive management, and sometimes it takes some investigation to discover who the real influencers are. This is especially true in matrix organizations.

- Key influencers usually have the profit-and-loss responsibility and/or authority to influence the areas of the organization that will be impacted.

- Key influencers are usually those who are able to allocate resources or able to clear the way for systemic or major structural implementation problems.

- Key influencers have some authority or influence over the areas where resistance is expected.

- There will always be multiple projects on the go, with overlapping and maybe conflicting or confusing elements. Key influencers will have the overview to sort this out and provide clear priorities.

- Really good implementation team leaders are always in high demand and short supply. Only the key influencers can prioritize and "pull rank" to free up these people who may be several levels below them.

Key influencers play a critical role in the leadership tower of support. Look for these characteristics to identify key influencers you can count on:

- They genuinely believe that the change to a new strategy is necessary.

- They understand the impact of the new strategy and realize the impact on the people, the organization, and the culture.

- They understand the risks, the total potential costs, the potential temporary dip in performance, and the time frame.

- They are willing to provide resources, make the management time commitment, and live through a potential temporary productivity loss.

- They need the new strategy in place so they can meet their objectives, or at a minimum they believe that the new initiatives are in their best interest (incentive/performance appraisal/compensation).

- They are expected to remain in their current position for the duration of the business-strategy implementation.

- They have the support of any governing body, such as the board of directors or parent company.

Launching a major strategy change without a strong leadership tower of support often results in a lack of resources, high frustration for the people involved, results that are slow to materialize, if ever, and in extreme cases, key people leaving the organization.

New Strategy Implementation Requires Project Management

If you approach your implementation project professionally, you will create the best possible results. The implementation management team—the drive team—will possess the right project-management and change-management expertise to keep the implementation project on an accelerated time line and ensure that the people in the organization adopt the new plan. On the other hand, if you communicate the new strategy and simply leave the details to "work themselves out," then obviously disaster is right around the corner. Here is a short checklist from experience:

- Manage this like any other project, with a plan, a schedule, and a budget and with organization, problem escalation, financial controls, document management, detailed actions, harmonization of performance measures, milestones, resources plans, and all that goes with good project management.

- Employee acceptance and adoption must be a top-level performance measurement for the implementation team. Consider that extra resources and actions need to be in place to communicate, get feedback, and listen to and resolve issues.

- Project management and change management require different, albeit overlapping, skill sets. Select the implementation leadership team—the drive team—with care.

- Normally the existing business must continue to operate while you are implementing the new business strategy. Consider several options to structure the implementation so that the interruption is minimized. Perhaps the project should run as a separate disconnected test group first. Perhaps there should be a parallel system for a period. Perhaps a phased-in approach can start with a pilot and systematically phase in portions of the organization. Is it best to have a onetime switch-over or a migration or a participatory approach as the organization accepts the new model? Each approach must consider the balance between the need to accelerate the implementation, the cost of lost productivity during the transition period, and the risk of a failed implementation if it is too quick and the organization fails to get back into operational mode.

- Highly complex changes (especially complex technology changes such as the implementation of enterprise-wide IT systems) need very tight project management. Without it the system is surely to miss deadlines and have severe cost overruns and ultimately may not be functional.

- Accelerated implementation usually means not everything can get done in the initial phases. Communicate that fact to everyone—tell them what will be done first and why. Prioritize the key success factors in the implementation and focus, focus, focus on the mission-critical aspects of large-scale adoption of the new strategy.

- Remember that the implementation project is not over until benefits are being realized.

Engage an Implementation Drive Team That Matches the Situation

Engage managers with the project-management and change-management experience that match the complexity and business situation. This is not a place to go cheap. This is the skill set that will ensure that the deliverables are delivered. Here is a short checklist from my experience:

- Although project managers are often assigned based on their experience with similar projects, look inside your organization for change-management experience. Change management requires a high familiarity with the organization's people and culture.

- Consider the level of complexity of the change required as a result of the new business strategy:

    o the extent of the organization involved

    o the number of levels of the organization involved

    o the number of functions, business units, or departments involved

    o the number of locations involved

    o the geographic spread of the locations involved

    o the speed of change required and the amount of transition time allowed

    o the resources available versus required (or ideal)

    o the extent of the change; operational change or enterprise-wide change or cultural change

    o the degree of job change required by individuals

- o the extent of the resistance, reluctance, and objections expected

- Consider the ability of the organization to digest change:

  - o A long-established and entrenched culture that has not gone through any significant change is likely to adopt slowly and have high resistance.

  - o A highly agile work culture with people who are accustomed to enterprise-wide change (and a high likelihood that there is a high portion of early adopters who we hope don't have transition burnout) will be more likely to accept the change readily.

  - o The weariness of the organization to change—have they gone through some major changes recently that are still being digested (process changes, job changes, culture acceptance)? Just like individuals, organizations can suffer change burnout. They need a stability period.

"The Devil Is in the Details"

Often the author of the new business strategy, a top executive, is not a "details person." The details are left to the implementation team, and it is only during the implementation that the true complexities of the change requirements come to light. It is only in the details of the project plan that you can ensure that processes, job functions, organization, resources, rewards, and infrastructure systems are aligned with the new business strategy.

It is only in the details of the implementation plan that you will discover processes that need to be rewritten or job functions that need to be created. The detailed discoveries of the implementation plan are critical to success and converting the new business strategy into a new functional and operational business.

Some resistance and design problems will only come to light when you execute the implementation plan. Be prepared to redesign and fine-tune as you go. Generally speaking, if the Compelling Attraction is well thought out and reasonably granular, the implementation team will be able to use the Compelling Attraction description as a guide to make fine-tuning decisions.

Strategy Implementation Requires Resources

If I have done nothing else in this book, I hope that I have given you an appreciation for some of the requirements of good implementation management. I think it is obvious that there are change-management, project-management, communication, and implementation activities that all require time and/or expenditures. There are also other indirect costs such as a slump in productivity caused by an increase in the amount of meetings, training, watercooler chitchat, confusion, and other distractions, such as employees who become minimally productive because they are preoccupied with potential job loss. All these direct and indirect costs are associated with the introduction and implementation of a new business strategy.

Accelerating the implementation may take a little more investment in preparation, but the overall cost does not have to be significantly higher. There are a few typical added costs associated with accelerating the implementation of the new strategy:

- the development of tools such as the Compelling Attraction and the 100-Second Enlightenment

- the time invested to make sure the leadership team is ready to actively supportive the new strategy and provide the necessary resources

- the diligent business plan review and the confirmation of its "critical bits"

It comes as no surprise that successfully implementing any new business strategy requires some investment in the implementation effort. After all, we are trying to overcome the stabilizing forces of the status quo. It also should come as no surprise that to accelerate the implementation requires some extra effort. The extra effort comes in the form of preparation, as mentioned above, and extra implementation effort. To overcome the status quo, a sudden and massive effort to change is very effective. It is usually preferable to the "trickle-down crusade" of traditional business-strategy implementation. Overall, the incremental investment to accelerate the implementation is usually modest compared to the standard traditional approach. Assuming that your new strategy is a winner, the added investment to accelerate the implementation will be quickly repaid with a quick launch of the new business approach.

Keep the Turmoil Period as Short as Possible

The most difficult period for the people in the organization and the period that has the highest risk of business performance loss is during the rollout of the new business strategy—the fluid transition or turmoil period. Keep it a short as possible.

The turmoil period is the time when the most confusion exists. This confusion can be minimized by many of the other tips included in this book, but there will always be some confusion in the turmoil period.

The acute turmoil period usually begins the day of the announcement or the rumors of an announcement. The turmoil typically peaks as people start to understand the changes required by the new plans and continues through the challenges of the rollout.

Here are a few observations from experience:

- The longer the turmoil period, the more likely people will lose their faith, drift back to old ways, feel insecure, and become systemically unproductive.

- The longer the turmoil period, the increased risk that your good people will leave. Competitors are always looking for good people, and these are exactly the people you need most.

- Put an aggressive implementation drive team in place to help ensure that the process is driven and not gravity fed. This is not the time to starve the process of resources. Lethargy is the enemy. The status quo is the competition.

- If the new business strategy initiates a wide comprehensive change, then a lot must be done in parallel to limit the chaotic transition period and to accelerate the implementation. This multiplies the complexity and requirement for preparation, coordination, communications, and resources.

- Balance the need for a short transition period with the time required for people to accept and understand the changes of the new business strategy.

The 100-Second Enlightenment and the Compelling Attraction of the new business model create excitement and energy in the organization. All this energy slowly evaporates. Use this energy as one of your implementation resources. Your task is to get through the turmoil before the energy evaporates.

Don't Overlook Basic Skill and Organizational Requirements

It may seem obvious, but it is worth saying. Make sure the people, skills, and organization fit the new business strategy. As part of the implementation process, you may want to include some kind of skills needs and gaps assessment. Also, take a fresh look at the organizational structure in light of the new business strategy. Usually any changes in the macro-view of the organization are considered and part of the new strategy. However, the local organizations are sometimes overlooked and end up not fitting the new approach.

Don't Forget to Change the Infrastructure

Don't forget about the infrastructure. There are many business support processes, systems, and functions that operate silently in the background. With a new business strategy some of this infrastructure may be impacted and need to be modified. This is easy to overlook, and just when you think the rollout has gone well, you find out that key parts of the infrastructure no longer support the new business approach and all the work that went into accelerating the implementation is lost by the delays caused by overlooked infrastructure changes. Every situation and organization will be different, but here is a sample list of potential infrastructure items that may be overlooked.

- organization and reporting lines

- business reporting

- communication systems

- job descriptions

- approval authorities for proposals, purchases, contracts, hiring, capital expenditures, expenses, overtime, vacation time, technical and commercial risk reviews, etc.

- emergency "who to call" lists

- emergency business resumption procedures

- on-call lists

- call center updates

- security requirements—physical and electronic

- distribution channel communication and procedures

- marketing materials—distribution and updates

- Web site information and updates

- advertising

- IT systems and e-mail systems

- order entry and financial data entry

- IT reporting and access

- communication methods with various groups, sales force, production staff, international staff, etc.

- sales territories and split recognition between territories

- agency or third-party agreements

- technical support

- credit review

- cash-flow management

- accounts receivable

- project-management or job-management systems' procedures, processes, tools

- acquisition and disposal of assets

- business planning and budgeting

- legal reviews

- registration with governing bodies

- executive committees

- corporate/central services

- maintenance systems—planning, scheduling, etc.

- production planning and scheduling

- inventory management systems, tools, procedures, processes, systems

- engineering approval and design changes

- drawing management, approval, signoff, data storage

- copyright and patent management—intellectual property management

- time-sheet authorization

- work assignment

- account assignment

- job planning

- material expediting

- incoming call handling, call routing, call handling, call-referral problem solving (incoming from telephone, Web site, or e-mail)

- problem escalation

- intra-organization dispute settlement and arbitration

- market research

- customer satisfaction—surveys, responses, inquiries

- quality programs

- office/facility management, heating and cooling system, snow removal, pest control

- recruiting, hiring, and new employee orientation

- training and development

- health and safety

- career planning and paths

- communication (internal, external, public relations, press releases, etc.)

- performance-appraisal process

- performance-measurement systems realignment

- compensation system/categories, progression, overtime, equality, incentives, etc.

- disciplinary processes

- benefits—content, communication to employees, interaction to engage benefits

Prepare for Obstacles

There will be problems, unexpected issues, and obstacles along the way. Expect them and put a fast escalation/resolution process in place. It may be simply a helpline or easy access to the drive team. The key is to acknowledge the issue and address it as quickly as possible. The people who are conscientious enough to notify you of a problem are the people who are driving the accelerated implementation. It demonstrates that they are trying to implement the business strategy. These are the people you want to motivate and keep motivated. Don't let them down. If you let them down, you will be doing more damage than simply not solving their issue. You will be de-motivating your champions and will risk evaporating the energy and the inertia you have created.

A Tactical Example

A number of years ago I was a core member of a team developing an asset-management service package that could be offered to large industrial customers. Once the development of the service package was completed and tested, we went to all the regional service offices to explain how the package worked and to teach the local team how to introduce it to their market. It was essentially a self-contained service offering that could be completely implemented by the local groups and promoted to their customers.

After some time, we found that there were only a few locations where the new service package took root and was being implemented. Some locations had implemented the new initiative and were generating income in a few months, while other locations had not implemented the new offering at all.

When we investigated we made a number of observations and learned a number of lessons:

- In the locations that implemented the new offering there was a champion who stepped into a leadership role and implemented the program. Each of these local leaders was creative and had the confidence to start the implementation. This local champion guided the others in that location as a drive team leader.

- In locations where no implementation took place, there was no drive team leader who felt confident enough or a person who felt they had the backup support to start the implementation—to "take the ball and run with it."

- As an organization, we learned a number of lessons from this:

  o The need for a more local support and more detailed information—more resources.

  o The level of detail required varies from individual to individual.

  o The need to identify a drive team leader and get agreement on a drive team implementation plan.

  o That there was a skill set missing—a lack of sales coverage in some areas.

  o That there was not enough follow-up training.

  o That contract management support was missing.

  o The collapse of the tower of management support. There were local service managers who did not believe that the service offering was necessary or beneficial. Consequently the implementation of the new plan was not a priority and no resources were assigned to support it.

That was many years ago. We learned our lessons and made corrections. The service package has since been introduced all around the world, and the company has had considerable success with it.

Part V

Embed the New Business Strategy

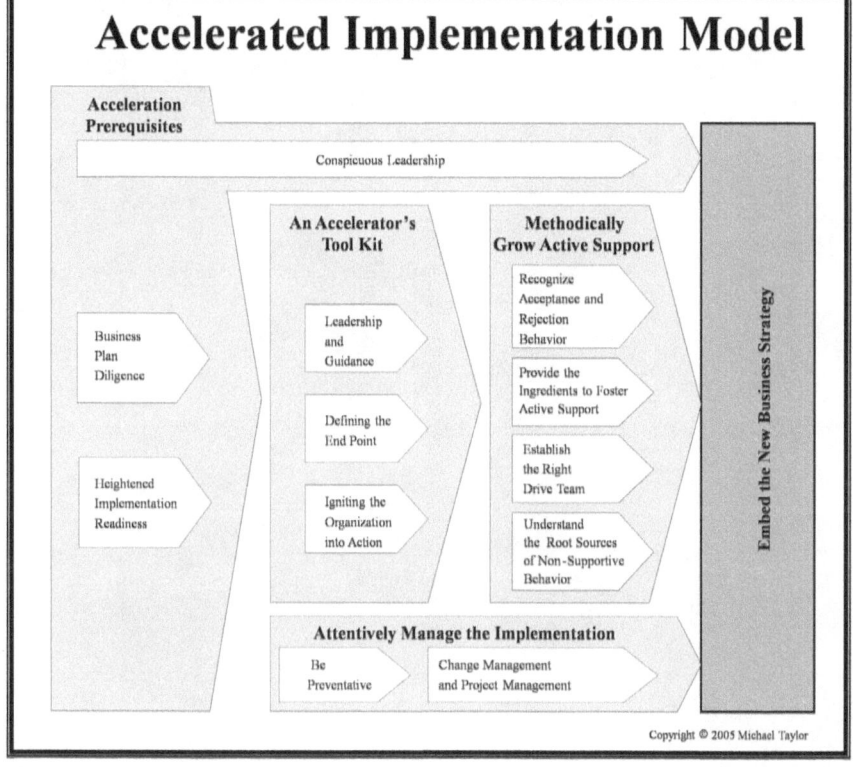

Accelerated Implementation Model

Acceleration Prerequisites

Conspicuous Leadership

An Accelerator's Tool Kit

Methodically Grow Active Support

Business Plan Diligence

Leadership and Guidance

Recognize Acceptance and Rejection Behavior

Provide the Ingredients to Foster Active Support

Defining the End Point

Establish the Right Drive Team

Heightened Implementation Readiness

Igniting the Organization into Action

Understand the Root Sources of Non-Supportive Behavior

Embed the New Business Strategy

Attentively Manage the Implementation

Be Preventative

Change Management and Project Management

Copyright © 2005 Michael Taylor

Chapter 13

Embed the New Business Strategy

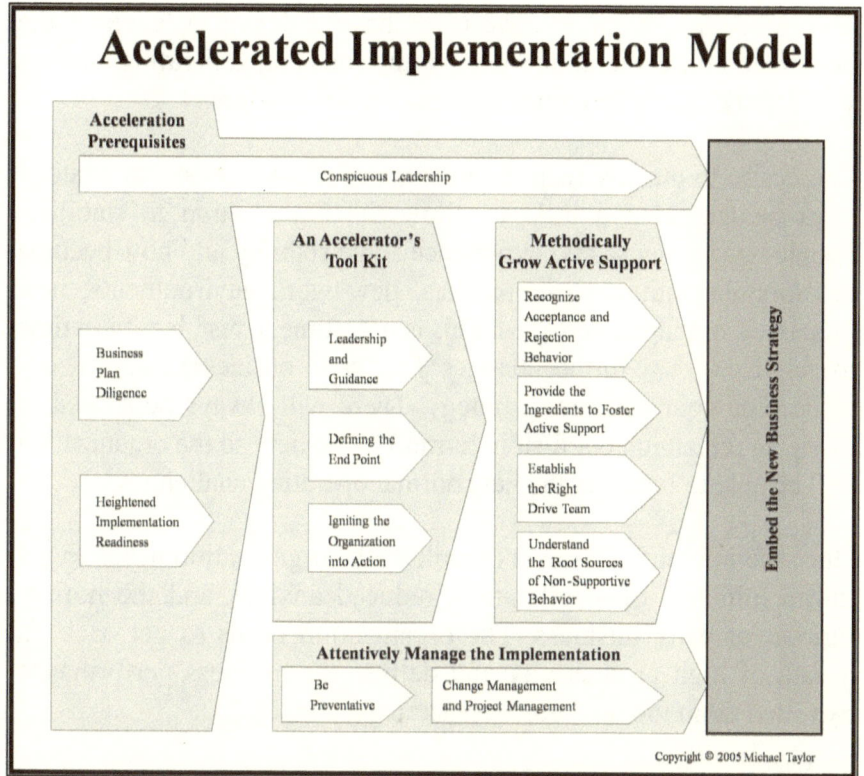

Accelerated Implementation Model

Acceleration Prerequisites

Conspicuous Leadership

An Accelerator's Tool Kit

Leadership and Guidance

Defining the End Point

Igniting the Organization into Action

Methodically Grow Active Support

Recognize Acceptance and Rejection Behavior

Provide the Ingredients to Foster Active Support

Establish the Right Drive Team

Understand the Root Sources of Non-Supportive Behavior

Business Plan Diligence

Heightened Implementation Readiness

Embed the New Business Strategy

Attentively Manage the Implementation

Be Preventative

Change Management and Project Management

Copyright © 2005 Michael Taylor

Changing from New to Normal

The conclusion of the new strategy implementation is a time of conflicting needs. We need to rest from the high-effort implementation activity while becoming comfortable with new business practices and quickly taking advantage of the investment in the new strategy to experience some success.

Implementing a new business strategy initiates change and in the process initiates a period of heightened activity, energy, confusion, turmoil, and anxiety during the implementation. Inexperienced managers sometimes foresee that once the new strategy is largely implemented there should be a feeling of "task accomplished" and a time to rest. On the contrary, usually this is no time to rest. It is usually a time to aggressively take advantage of new market opportunities or to catch competition before any more ground is lost. As senior managers, we often have a desire to leverage the heightened implementation energy and focus on generating success while working out any final implementation matters.

The desire to quickly reap the rewards of the new business strategy must be tempered a little to allow the organization to stabilize. People need to sense and experience some stability and now become comfortable with new approaches, new work environments, new processes, or maybe new jobs. This is not a time to rest, but it is a time to stabilize with no further changes. The "new" business strategy needs to become "our" business strategy. There will always be a need to dissipate remaining confusion, turmoil, or anxiety so the organization will be able to focus on the new normal operating challenges.

Once the implementation is complete, the organization needs to get into a mind-set of stabilization, reduced anxiety, and the normal turmoil of daily business. The organization needs to get back on a path of high productivity and deliver the business performance expected from the new business strategy.

There is a balance required. On one hand you need to stabilize the organization. On the other hand you need to quickly leverage the new business strategy. In this section we have a few ideas from experience to help embed the new business strategy, make it stick, and transition from "implementing the new strategy" to "normal operating mode."

Don't Lose Sight of Reality and the Real Implementation Status

Don't be premature with your completion announcements. It is easy for senior management to lose sight of "on-the-ground" implementation status. Senior managers naturally focus on macro rather than micro issues and focus on longer-term issues rather than the nitty-gritty progress of tactical issues. In addition, senior managers may feel that it seems like a long time ago since the initial implementation initiatives were launched. Much of the implementation activity may be "under the radar" of senior managers. Consequently, senior managers can sometimes run the risk of falsely believing that the implementation of the new business strategy is substantially complete when in reality, process changes and job function changes are still taking effect. From a high level the implementation may seem substantially complete, but be cautious and double-check the true situation. In reality, mission-critical implementation activities may still be underway.

If people in the organization have unresolved objections to the new business strategy or reluctance to actively support the implementation and rollout, this may be an indication that it is premature to announce success. You will likely never get 100 percent of the people supporting any strategy, but you need more than a simple majority. You need the support of an overwhelming majority to consider the implementation substantially complete. Make sure support is not just lip service. Some people say they have accepted new ideas, processes, or tools; however, they never actually implement them. Some implement superficially and you will never really get the benefits desired … not to mention that it sets a new standard of mediocrity. Look for the proof of implementation.

Why is it such a big deal to make sure you are substantially complete before announcing success? By announcing that the new business strategy is substantially implemented, you may reduce the anxiety associated with a period of change and turmoil, but you may also simultaneously reduce the energy associated with the drive to completion. By announcing substantial completion, you are creating a perception that the existing status of completion is "good enough" even if it is far from complete. Make sure you are truly substantially complete before pronouncing completion.

Entrench Each Stage or Major Portion of the New Model

At the right point, announce the completion of each major portion of the new business strategy. There may be phases that can be celebrated or functional areas of the company that can be celebrated. People need to begin to see the progress. It is important at some time to declare victory, even if it is a victory over portions or segments of the new business strategy.

Consider removing the old processes and infrastructure support (of course after the new system is running and reliable). Remember that you are always paddling upstream and that some people will want to drift back to the old methods. By removing the infrastructure and/ or their ability to move back, you entrench a growing portion of the new system.

Communicate for Entrenchment—Stop Calling It New

Communication continues to be critical for some time until the new model is considered the norm. Stop calling it the "new" business strategy and start referring to it as "our" business strategy. Continue to communicate successes—don't shortcut a growing list of success stories. Demonstrate more success than before the change. Use any new language or terminology that was created by the new business strategy in communications so that it becomes part of the norm.

Celebrate Success and Energize the New Business Strategy

Nothing says success like a celebration. It is a time when the contributions of everyone can be recognized and everyone can take some satisfaction in the implementation of the new strategy and have some fun. If it is appropriate to have the leadership give an address at the party, then it is a good time to put the new strategy in the perspective of the history, highlight the accomplishments of the organization, and paint a motivating picture of the future.

Publicly congratulate the successful completion of the launch of the new business strategy. This will help squash some of the lingering thoughts about retreating to the old status quo business approach. Hopefully it will extinguish any lingering reluctance to accept the new plan.

Give people the recognition of success. Celebrate as a group to help unite the organization in the new business environment. It is also comforting for them to know that the anxiety and confusion of the implementation period is over and gives some closure to the period of change and turmoil and allows them to stabilize their new work habits.

Calibrate Your Expectations of Culture Change

I want to close this chapter with some thoughts about culture change. Culture change is the sum of many changes … it is actions, not policy. Culture change is not a new color logo. Culture is described as "the way we do things around here" … the norm. Culture change takes time.

Simply announcing a new business strategy, training everyone, and launching the change associated with the new strategy does not change culture. Make sure the people are genuinely trying to work through the problems, using the tools, getting the benefits, and living the new model. You cannot prescribe culture. You can simply provide the ingredients to promote desired traits of a culture, such as a reward system, that motivates desired behavior or a structure that organizes desired working groups to interact together. Culture is a result of the values and the behavior of the people in the organization, including the management team.

The organization's culture is the organization's personality. Changing it implies certain truths.

- Culture change does not happen overnight.

- People must be motivated and want to accept the new characteristics of the organization's new personality.

- People need the tools to help implement the desired changes.

- People often need coaching; culture/personality change is not routine, and people are not sure what to do. Some people do not deal with abstract situations very well.

- The change needs to be engrained or entrenched to be the new norm/habit before the change is done. The entrenchment takes time before it is really rooted.

Calibrate your expectations of the desired outcomes and the speed of culture change.

A Closing Comment

Implementing a new business strategy can be complicated and fraught with frustration and risk for your career. On the other hand it can be rewarding, generate newfound success for your organization, and put your career into overdrive. The key is to have a game plan that will help avoid pitfalls, generate enthusiasm, and accelerate the adoption of your new ideas.

If you can embed some of the ideas we discussed in your organization so that these ideas become normal practice, you can generate organizational agility—one of the most sought after competitive advantages in business today.

Enjoy your success.

Suggested Reading

Covey, Stephen. *The 7 Habits of Highly Effective People*. New York: Fireside, 1990.

"Culture and Change." *Harvard Business Review*. Boston: Harvard Business School, 2002.

Duck, Jeanie Daniel. *The Change Monster*. New York: Crown Business, 2001.

Fullan, Michael. *Leading in a Culture of Change*. San Francisco: Jossey-Bass, 2001.

Gardner, Howard. *Changing Minds*. Boston: Harvard Business School Press, 2004.

Knowles, Malcolm, et al. *The Adult Learner*. Woburn, MA: Butterworth-Heinemann, 1998.

Kotter, John. *The Heart of Change*. Boston: Harvard Business School Press, 2002.

Kotter, John. *Leading Change*. Boston: Harvard Business School Press, 1996.

Kriegel, Robert, and David Brandt. *Sacred Cows Make the Best Burgers*. New York: Warner, 1997.

McCarthy, Bernice. *About Learning*. Barrington, IL: Excel, 1996.

Ryans, Adrian, et al. *Winning Market Leadership*. San Francisco: John Wiley and Sons, 1999.

Senge, Peter. *The Fifth Discipline*. New York: Currency Doubleday, 1994.

About the Author

Michael Taylor is a member of the Marketing Management Faculty at the Richard Ivey School of Business at the University of Western Ontario, in London, Ontario, Canada. Prior to joining the university, Michael Taylor has twenty years' experience in various management roles with large international companies and has been responsible for managing the execution of a wide range of strategic and business-development projects. He has been an advisor to senior executives. He has played a critical role in accelerating the implementation of a number of business initiatives. He has examined the reasons why some initiatives succeed, even with major impediments, while others flounder. Mr. Taylor has studied change management and combined this core knowledge with his own research, observations, and his own practical experience. It was from this understanding that Mr. Taylor developed the *Accelerated Implementation Model (AIM)*. Throughout *Accelerating Business*, Mr. Taylor provides examples from his own experience.

Mr. Taylor began his career in 1981 as a service technician after completing studies in electrical control systems technology at Fanshawe College in London, Ontario, Canada. He also holds a bachelor's degree in economics from the University of Western Ontario and a master's degree in business administration from the prestigious Ivey School of Business. Mr. Taylor has held a number of progressively responsible positions, including national marketing manager and senior manager of strategic development.

Mr. Taylor has extensive experience managing projects with complex organizational dimensions. He has played a senior role in a wide range of complex projects, including designing the integration of the business systems of a newly acquired company; developing and commercializing patented asset-management programs; and leading key aspects of complex reorganizations, the implementation of new go-to-market strategies, the implementation of customer-relationship management (CRM) systems, and accelerating the success of national account-management programs.

www.ingramcontent.com/pod-product-compliance
Lightning Source LLC
Chambersburg PA
CBHW032004170526
45157CB00002B/544